TEACHER'S PET PUBLICATIONS

LITPLAN TEACHER PACK
for
The Indian in the Cupboard
based on the book by
Lynne Reid Banks

Written by
Debra Lemieux

© 2008 Teacher's Pet Publications
All Rights Reserved

Copyright Teacher's Pet Publications 2008

Only the student materials in this unit plan (such as worksheets, study questions, and tests) may be reproduced multiple times for use in the purchaser's classroom.

For any additional copyright questions, contact Teacher's Pet Publications.

www.tpet.com

TABLE OF CONTENTS - *The Indian in the Cupboard*

Introduction	5
Unit Objectives	7
Reading Assignment Sheet	8
Unit Outline	9
Study Questions (Short Answer)	13
Quiz/Study Questions (Multiple Choice)	21
Pre-reading Vocabulary Worksheets	39
Lesson One (Introductory Lesson)	57
Oral Reading Evaluation Form	65
Writing Assignment #1	67
Writing Assignment #2	72
Writing Assignment #3	78
Writing Evaluation Form	69
Non-fiction Assignment Sheet	77
Extra Discussion Questions/Writing Assignments	87
Vocabulary Review Activities	92
Unit Review Activities	93
Unit Tests	99
Unit Resource Materials	147
Vocabulary Resource Materials	165

ABOUT THE AUTHOR

Lynne Reid Banks

Lynne Reid Banks has written numerous books for both children and adults. She is best known for the children's novel *The Indian in the Cupboard,* which has sold over 10 million copies and was made into a film.

Banks an only child was born in London in 1929. During World War II she evacuated to Canada but returned to London when the war was over. Before her writing career Banks was an actress, and was one of the first women to work as a television journalist in Britain. In 1962 Banks emigrated to Israel and married Chaim Stephenson. They had three sons and returned to England in 1971.

Banks currently lives in Dorset with her husband.

CHILDREN'S NOVELS INCLUDE:

The Indian in the Cupboard Series:
The Indian in the Cupboard
The Return of the Indian
The Secret of the Indian
The Mystery of the Cupboard
The Key to the Indian

OTHER WORKS INCLUDE:
Tiger Tiger
The Adventures of King Midas
Alice-By-Accident
Angela and Diabola
The Dungeon
Maura's Angel
One More River
Broken Bridge
The Fairy Rebel
The Farthest-Away Mountain
Harry the Poisonous Centipede
Harry the Poisonous Centipede Goes To Sea
Harry the Poisonous Centipede's Big Adventure
I, Houdini
Stealing Stacey
Melusine

INTRODUCTION *The Indian in the Cupboard*

This LitPlan has been designed to develop students' reading, writing, thinking, and language skills through exercises and activities related to *The Indian in the Cupboard*. It includes twenty-one lessons, supported by extra resource materials.

The **introductory lesson** introduces students to the concept of friendship. Following the introductory activity, students are given a transition to explain how the activity relates to the book they are about to read. Following the transition, students are given the materials they will be using during the unit. As a class, preview the study guide questions and vocabulary worksheet, and begin reading the novel.

The **reading assignments** are approximately thirty pages each; some are a little shorter while others are a little longer. Students have approximately 15 minutes of pre-reading work to do prior to each reading assignment. This pre-reading work involves reviewing the study questions for the assignment and doing some vocabulary work for selected vocabulary words they will encounter in their reading.

The **study guide questions** are fact-based questions; students can find the answers to these questions right in the text. These questions come in two formats: short answer or multiple choice. The best use of these materials is probably to use the short answer version of the questions as study guides for students (since answers will be more complete), and to use the multiple choice version for occasional quizzes.

The **vocabulary work** is intended to enrich students' vocabularies as well as to aid in the students' understanding of the book. Prior to each reading assignment, students will complete a two-part worksheet for selected vocabulary words in the upcoming reading assignment. Part I focuses on the students' use of general knowledge and contextual clues by giving the sentence in which the word appears in the text. Students are then to write down what they think the words mean based on the words' usage. Part II nails down the definitions of the words by giving students dictionary definitions of the words and having students match the words to the correct definitions based on the words' contextual usage. Students should then have an understanding of the words when they meet them in the text.

After each reading assignment, students will go back and formulate answers for the study guide questions. Discussion of these questions serves as a **review** of the most important events and ideas presented in the reading assignments.

After students have completed reading the work, there is a **vocabulary review** lesson which pulls together all of the fragmented vocabulary lists for the reading assignments and gives students a review of all of the words they have studied.

Following the vocabulary review, a lesson is devoted to the **extra discussion questions/writing assignments.** These questions focus on interpretation, critical analysis, and personal response, employing a variety of thinking skills and adding to the students' understanding of the novel.

There is a **group theme project** in this unit in which students will research Indians, cowboys, or pioneers and present their findings to the class.

There are three **writing assignments** in this unit, each with the purpose of persuading, informing, or writing to entertain. In the first assignment, students write a persuasive letter that convinces one of the book's characters to keep his secret *or* convinces him to tell someone. In the second assignment, students compose an original folktale. In the third assignment students will write an essay from the information they gathered in the group assignment.

There is a **non-fiction reading assignment** that ties in with the group project. Students must read non-fiction magazines, books, etc. to gather information about Indians, cowboys, or pioneers.

The **review lesson** pulls together all of the aspects of the unit. The teacher is given four or five choices of activities or games to use which all serve the same basic function of reviewing all of the information presented in the unit.

The **unit tests** come in two formats: multiple choice or short answer. As a convenience, two different tests for each format have been included. There is also an advanced short answer unit test for advanced students.

There are additional **support materials** included with this unit. The **Unit Resource Materials** section includes suggestions for an in-class library, crossword and word search puzzles related to the novel, and extra worksheets. There is a list of **bulletin board ideas** which gives the teacher suggestions for bulletin boards to go along with this unit. In addition, there is a list of **extra class activities** the teacher could choose from to enhance the unit or as a substitution for an exercise the teacher might feel is inappropriate for his/her class. **Answer keys** are located directly after the **reproducible materials** throughout the unit. The **Vocabulary Resource Materials** section includes similar worksheets and games to reinforce the vocabulary words.

The **level** of this unit can be varied depending upon the criteria on which the individual assignments are graded, the teacher's expectations of his/her students in class discussions, and the formats chosen for the study guides, quizzes and test. If teachers have other ideas/activities they wish to use, they can usually easily be inserted prior to the review lesson. The student materials may be reproduced for use in the teacher's classroom without infringement of copyrights. No other portion of this unit may be reproduced without the written consent of Teacher's Pet Publications, Inc.

UNIT OBJECTIVES *The Indian in the Cupboard*

1. Through reading Lynne Reid Banks's *The Indian in the Cupboard,* students will reflect upon friendship and how it evolves and changes over time.

2. Students will demonstrate their understanding of the text on four levels: factual, interpretive, critical, and personal.

3. Students will be given the opportunity to practice reading orally and silently to improve their skills in each area.

4. Students will answer questions to demonstrate their knowledge and understanding of the main events and characters in *The Indian in the Cupboard* as they relate to the author's theme development.

5. Students will enrich their vocabularies and improve their understanding of the novel through the vocabulary lessons prepared for use in conjunction with the novel.

6. The writing assignments in this unit are geared to several purposes:
    a. To have students demonstrate their abilities to inform, to persuade, or to express their own personal ideas

    Note: Students will demonstrate the ability to write effectively to inform by developing and organizing facts to convey information. Students will demonstrate the ability to write effectively to persuade by selecting and organizing relevant information, establishing an argumentative purpose, and by designing an appropriate strategy for an identified audience. Students will demonstrate the ability to write effectively to express personal ideas by selecting a form and its appropriate elements.

    b. To check the students' reading comprehension
    c. To make students think about the ideas presented by the novel
    d. To encourage logical thinking
    e. To provide an opportunity to practice good grammar and improve students' use of the English language

7. Students will read orally, report, and participate in large and small group discussions to improve their public speaking and personal interaction skills.

READING ASSIGNMENTS *The Indian in the Cupboard*

Date Assigned	Assignment	Completion Date
	Assignment #1 Chapters 1-2	
	Assignment #2 Chapters 3-5	
	Assignment #3 Chapters 6-7	
	Assignment #4 Chapters 8-9	
	Assignment #5 Chapters 10-12	
	Assignment #6 Chapters 13-14	
	Assignment #7 Chapters 15-16	

UNIT OUTLINE *The Indian in the Cupboard*

1 Introduction PVR Ch. 1-2	2 Study ? Ch. 1-2 Legends, Myths, Folktales	3 Legends, Myths, Legends Group Reports	4 PVR Ch. 3-5 Oral Reading	5 Study ? Ch.3-5 Writing Assignment #1
6 PVR 6-7 Complete Writing Assignment #1	7 Study ? Ch. 6-7 Writing Assignment #2	8 PVR 8-9	9 Study ? Ch. 8-9 Introduce Group Project Non-fiction Writing Assignment #3	10 PVR 10-12
11 Study ? Ch. 10-12	12 PVR 13-14	13 Study ? Ch. 13-14 Group Work	14 PVR 15-16	15 Study ? Ch. 15-16 Group Work
16 Extra Discussion ?s	17 Group Work	18 Group Project Presentations	19 Vocabulary Review	20 Unit Review
21 Unit Tests				

Key: P = Preview Study Questions   V = Vocabulary Work   R = Read

STUDY GUIDE QUESTIONS

STUDY GUIDE QUESTIONS *The Indian in the Cupboard*

Assignment #1
Chapters 1-2
1. What is Patrick's birthday gift to Omri?
2. Why is Omri happy to receive the white metal cupboard from Gillon?
3. What is special about the key Omri finds to lock the cupboard?
4. When Omri discovers the live Indian in the cupboard, why does he decide to keep it a secret?
5. What is Omri's reaction when the Indian threatens to kill Omri if he touches the Indian?
6. After Omri drops several tantalizing hints to Patrick about Little Bear, what is Patrick's reaction?
7. Before going to breakfast Omri locks the Indian back in the cupboard and does not return to it until after school. What does Omri discover when he opens the cupboard?
8. What does Omri do when the Indian asks for food?
9. How does the Indian introduce himself?
10. Where does Little Bear sleep during his first night with Omri?

Assignment #2
Chapters 3-5
1. What elements together magically bring toys to life?
2. Why does Omri consider turning Little Bear back into plastic?
3. What does Little Bear tell Omri when he asks if Little Bear has a wife?
4. Why does Omri take Little Bear and his horse outside?
5. When Little Bear realizes all the dangers outside, what does he request from Omri?
6. Why does Omri bring the First World War soldier to life?
7. What does the soldier think of Omri?
8. What type of house does Little Bear want to build?
9. Why does Omri place a knight inside the cupboard?

Assignment #3
Chapters 6-7
1. Why does Omri use part of his lunch money to buy the Indian chief?
2. What shocks Omri about the Indian chief?
3. What has Omri done to make his father angry?
4. Why does Omri tell Patrick about Little Bear?
5. Omri runs into Patrick when he comes out of the hardware store. What does Patrick have for Omri?
6. Why is Omri upset that his brothers are in his room when he returns from the hardware store?
7. What is Patrick's reaction when he sees Little Bear for the first time?
8. What things worry Omri?

9. How does Little Bear cook his steak?

Assignment #4
Chapters 8-9

1. What spoils Little Bear's steak dinner?
2. What does Patrick do when Omri leaves his room to get Little Bear something else for his dinner?
3. What is Omri afraid will happen if Little Bear and the cowboy meet?
4. Patrick agrees to let Omri take care of his cowboy the first night, but what does he threaten to do if Omri puts the cowboy back in the cupboard or does not bring him to school the next day?
5. Where does Omri decide to keep the cowboy and his horse the first night?
6. What does the cowboy do that upsets Omri?
7. What does Omri have to do to get Little Bear to dance?
8. What sound wakes Omri up at dawn?
9. How does the cowboy escape from the crate?
10. How does Omri convince Little Bear not to kill the cowboy?
11. What is Boone's nickname? Why?

Assignment #5
Chapters 10-12

1. How does Omri get Boone to eat breakfast with Little Bear?
2. After breakfast Boone and Little Bear fight. How does Omri stop the fight?
3. Why does Omri bring Boone and Little Bear an egg cup filled with hot water?
4. What does Omri tell Boone and Little Bear will happen if they are seen at school?
5. What happens outside the school when Omri gives Boone to Patrick?
6. What makes Omri let out a short yelp in the main hall?
7. At lunch Omri gives Boone and Little Bear to Patrick. What does Omri tell Patrick he will do if anything happens to Little Bear?
8. Why do Patrick and Omri get sent to Mr. Johnson, the headmaster's office?
9. Why does Omri knock Patrick down, sit on his chest, and pin Patrick's hands to the ground in Mr. Johnson's office?
10. What happens after Mr. Johnson throws Omri out of his office?

Assignment #6
Chapters 13-14

1. What condition are Little Bear and Boone in when Patrick gives them back to Omri in the bathroom?
2. Why doesn't Omri give Boone and Little Bear back to Patrick?
3. During art class, what does Omri learn about Boone?
4. Why does Omri burst out laughing when he leaves his art class?
5. Who stands up for Omri when Mr. Yapp accuses him of stealing?

6. Why does Adiel take the cupboard from Omri's room?
7. When Omri gets the cupboard back, why is it's magic gone?
8. What happens to Boone while he and Little Bear are watching a Western on TV?
9. Who removes the arrow from Boone's chest?
10. What happens to Little Bear's headdress?

Assignment #7
Chapters 15-16
1. Why does Omri move the seed box and Boone's bed up off the floor?
2. Why does Omri put Little Bear under the floor in his bedroom?
3. Why does Patrick ask if Little Bear has his bow and arrows with him under the floor?
4. Why is Omri so worried about Little Bear and Gillon's rat?
5. When Little Bear returns with the key what does Omri do?
6. What had not yet been discovered in Tommy's time?
7. Why does Little Bear get angry when Boone finds out it was Little Bear who shot him?
8. Why does Little Bear give Omri his belt made of white beads?
9. What makes Omri realize he needs to send Little Bear, his wife, and Boone back to their own time?
10. After Omri puts Little Bear, his wife, and Boone in the cupboard, why does Little Bear ask for Omri's hand?
11. What does Omri's mother tell him she will do with the key when he asks her to keep it for him?

STUDY GUIDE QUESTIONS ANSWER KEY *The Indian in the Cupboard*

Assignment #1
Chapters 1-2
1. What is Patrick's birthday gift to Omri?
   Patrick gives Omri a secondhand plastic Indian.
2. Why is Omri happy to receive the white metal cupboard from Gillon?
   Omri loves cupboards of any sort because it is fun to keep things in them.
3. What is special about the key Omri finds to lock the cupboard?
   The key was to his great-grandmother's jewel box. Omri's mother had worn it around her neck until the ribbon broke, and she almost lost it.
4. When Omri discovers the live Indian in the cupboard, why does he decide to keep it a secret?
   Omri is afraid if he takes his eyes off the Indian he will vanish, and his family will laugh and accuse him of telling lies. He also feels if the Indian is really alive, this is the most marvelous thing that has ever happened to him, and he wants to keep it to himself, at least at first.
5. What is Omri's reaction when the Indian threatens to kill Omri if he touches the Indian?
   Even though there is a vast difference in their sizes and strengths, Omri respects the Indian and is afraid.
6. After Omri drops several tantalizing hints to Patrick about Little Bear, what is Patrick's reaction?
   Patrick asks Omri if he is being sarcastic and then he tells Omri he doesn't believe him.
7. Before going to breakfast Omri locks the Indian back in the cupboard and does not return to it until after school. What does Omri discover when he opens the cupboard?
   He finds the Indian lying on the floor of the cupboard, and he is plastic again.
8. What does Omri do when the Indian asks for food?
   Omri sneaks into the kitchen and gets the Indian corn, bread, and cheese to eat and Coke to drink.
9. How does the Indian introduce himself?
   He points at himself proudly and says, "Little Bear. Iroquois brave. Son of chief."
10. Where does Little Bear sleep during his first night with Omri?
    He sleeps in a tepee made by Omri with a blanket cut from Omri's sweater.

Assignment #2
Chapters 3-5
1. What elements together magically bring toys to life?
   The toys must be plastic and the cupboard must be locked with Omri's great-grandmother's key.
2. Why does Omri consider turning Little Bear back into plastic?
   After a discussion of war and scalping, Omri realizes that Little Bear is real, not a toy or an actor.
3. What does Little Bear tell Omri when he asks if Little Bear has a wife?
   Little Bear tells Omri his wife is dead.
4. Why does Omri take Little Bear and his horse outside?
   Little Bear wants to ride his horse on the ground, not on the carpet.

5. When Little Bear realizes all the dangers outside, what does he request from Omri?
   Little Bear asks Omri for Indian weapons: bow, arrows, and a club. He also asks for a gun.
6. Why does Omri bring the First World War soldier to life?
   The soldier is a medical orderly and Omri needs a bandage the right size for Little Bear's leg.
7. What does the soldier think of Omri?
   The soldier thinks Omri is a dream.
8. What type of house does Little Bear want to build?
   He wants to build a longhouse.
9. Why does Omri place a knight inside the cupboard?
   He wants to give Little Bear the knight's battle-ax.

Assignment #3
Chapters 6-7
1. Why does Omri use part of his lunch money to buy the Indian chief?
   He buys the Indian chief for the bow and arrows to give to Little Bear.
2. What shocks Omri about the Indian chief?
   The Indian chief dies right after Omri brings him to life.
3. What has Omri done to make his father angry?
   Omri has taken a seed tray from his father's greenhouse and cut bark off the birch tree.
4. Why does Omri tell Patrick about Little Bear?
   Omri doesn't want to lose Patrick's friendship. He also wants to show someone else his Indian.
5. Omri runs into Patrick when he comes out of the hardware store. What does Patrick have for Omri?
   Patrick has a plastic cowboy on a horse.
6. Why is Omri upset that his brothers are in his room when he returns from the hardware store?
   Omri is afraid the boys will discover Little Bear or that the rat will injure him.
7. What is Patrick's reaction when he sees Little Bear for the first time?
   Patrick swallows, his eyes seem in danger of popping out of his head, and he doesn't speak when Little Bear speaks to him.
8. What things worry Omri?
   He doesn't want anyone else to find out about Little Bear. He wants Little Bear to be safe. He doesn't want to lose Patrick's friendship.
9. How does Little Bear cook his steak?
   He cooks it over a fire on a spit Omri makes with pieces from his erector set.

Assignment #4
Chapters 8-9
1. What spoils Little Bear's steak dinner?
   Omri and Patrick argue and Omri shoves Patrick causing him to tip the plate, spilling the fire on the carpet and making the meat roll under Omri's foot.
2. What does Patrick do when Omri leaves his room to get Little Bear something else for his dinner?
   Patrick puts the plastic cowboy and his horse in the cupboard.

3. What is Omri afraid will happen if Little Bear and the cowboy meet?
   Omri is afraid they will kill each other.
4. Patrick agrees to let Omri take care of his cowboy the first night, but what does he threaten to do if Omri puts the cowboy back in the cupboard or does not bring him to school the next day?
   Patrick threatens to tell about Little Bear and the cowboy.
5. Where does Omri decide to keep the cowboy and his horse the first night?
   Omri cleans out the dressing-up crate and puts the cowboy and his horse in there for the night.
6. What does the cowboy do that upsets Omri?
   The cowboy cries, and Omri does not know what to do.
7. What does Omri have to do to get Little Bear to dance?
   Omri must get Little Bear a wife and then he will dance.
8. What sound wakes Omri up at dawn?
   He hears shots.
9. How does the cowboy escape from the crate?
   The cowboy pushes out (or perhaps the horse kicks) a knot in the wood, leaving an oval-shaped hole like an arched doorway.
10. How does Omri convince Little Bear not to kill the cowboy?
    Omri tells Little Bear he will not get him a wife if he kills the cowboy.
11. What is Boone's nickname? Why?
    Boone's nickname is Boohoo because he cries so easily.

Assignment #5
Chapters 10-12

1. How does Omri get Boone to eat breakfast with Little Bear?
   Omri threatens to tell Little Bear Boone's nickname.
2. After breakfast Boone and Little Bear fight. How does Omri stop the fight?
   Omri pins both men down with his finger and tells them the fight is a draw.
3. Why does Omri bring Boone and Little Bear an egg cup filled with hot water?
   He wants them to bathe before he takes them to school.
4. What does Omri tell Boone and Little Bear will happen if they are seen at school?
   Omri tells them they could be taken away from Omri and then they would not be able to get back to their own time.
5. What happens outside the school when Omri gives Boone to Patrick?
   A nasty little girl named April sees Omri pass something to Patrick and brings this to the other children's attention. Soon Omri and Patrick are surrounded by the other children. Omri wants to bash them all, but the best he can do is barge through the chanting children with Patrick hot on his heels.
6. What makes Omri let out a short yelp in the main hall?
   Little Bear jabs Omri with his knife.
7. At lunch Omri gives Boone and Little Bear to Patrick. What does Omri tell Patrick he will do if anything happens to Little Bear?
   Omri says, "If you let anything happen to Little Bear, I will bash you so hard your teeth will fall out."
8. Why do Patrick and Omri get sent to Mr. Johnson, the headmaster's office?
   Patrick is late for class, and Omri is sent to Mr. Johnson for talking in class.

9. Why does Omri knock Patrick down, sit on his chest, and pin Patrick's hands to the ground in Mr. Johnson's office?
   Omri doesn't want Patrick to show Boone and Little Bear to Mr. Johnson.
10. What happens after Mr. Johnson throws Omri out of his office?
    Patrick shows Little Bear to Mr. Johnson.

Assignment #6
Chapters 13-14
1. What condition are Little Bear and Boone in when Patrick gives them back to Omri in the bathroom?
   Little Bear and Boone are terrified, clinging to each other. Even Little Bear is hiding his face.
2. Why doesn't Omri give Boone and Little Bear back to Patrick?
   Omri tells Patrick they are not safe with him. He says Patrick uses them and "you can't use people."
3. During art class, what does Omri learn about Boone?
   Art was Boone's best subject when he was in school, and he can draw very well.
4. Why does Omri burst out laughing when he leaves his art class?
   He has fooled his art teacher by pretending Boone's drawing is his own original creation.
5. Who stands up for Omri when Mr. Yapp accuses him of stealing?
   Patrick stands up for Omri.
6. Why does Adiel take the cupboard from Omri's room?
   Adiel got detention for not having his football shorts. He thinks Omri has taken them, so he takes the cupboard to teach Omri a lesson.
7. When Omri gets the cupboard back, why is it's magic gone?
   The key is missing.
8. What happens to Boone while he and Little Bear are watching a Western on TV?
   Angered by the killing of Indians in the Western TV show, Little Bear shoots Boone with an arrow.
9. Who removes the arrow from Boone's chest?
   Little Bear removes the arrow because Omri and Patrick are too big to do it safely.
10. What happens to Little Bear's headdress?
    Little Bear throws it on the ground and jumps on it, breaking all the feathers.

Assignment #7
Chapters 15-16
1. Why does Omri move the seed box and Boone's bed up off the floor?
   Gillon's rat is loose, and Omri is afraid for Boone and Little Bear.
2. Why does Omri put Little Bear under the floor in his bedroom?
   Omri realizes the missing key must have fallen through the floor, and he asks Little Bear to find it.
3. Why does Patrick ask if Little Bear has his bow and arrows with him under the floor?
   Patrick wants to know if Little Bear can defend himself from Gillon's rat.
4. Why is Omri so worried about Little Bear and Gillon's rat?
   Omri knows he will never forgive himself if Little Bear is killed.

5. When Little Bear returns with the key what does Omri do?
   Omri immediately brings Tommy (the medical orderly) back to life to help Boone.

6. What had not yet been discovered in Tommy's time?
   Penicillin had not been discovered.

7. Why does Little Bear get angry when Boone finds out it was Little Bear who shot him?
   Little Bear gets angry because Boone is more concerned with what happened in the TV show between the settlers and the Indians.

8. Why does Little Bear give Omri his belt made of white beads?
   He gives Omri the belt as payment for his new wife.

9. What makes Omri realize he needs to send Little Bear, his wife, and Boone back to their own time?
   When Little Bear tells Omri what he wants for his wedding, Omri realizes Little Bear will be happier in his own time.

10. After Omri puts Little Bear, his wife, and Boone in the cupboard, why does Little Bear ask for Omri's hand?
    Before going back to his own time Little Bear wants to make Omri his blood brother.

11. What does Omri's mother tell him she will do with the key when he asks her to keep it for him?
    She tells him she will get a chain and wear it like she always meant to.

MULTIPLE CHOICE STUDY/QUIZ QUESTIONS
The Indian in the Cupboard

Assignment #1
Chapters 1-2

1. What is Patrick's birthday gift to Omri?
    A. Patrick gives Omri a plastic cowboy on a horse.
    B. Patrick give Omri a secondhand plastic World War soldier.
    C. Patrick gives Omri a secondhand plastic Indian.
    D. Patrick gives Omri a white metal cupboard.

2. Why is Omri happy to receive the white metal cupboard from Gillon?
    A. Omri will keep all his medication in it.
    B. Omri loves cupboards of any sort because it is fun to keep things in them.
    C. Gillon has never given Omri a gift, so he is happy to get anything from Gillon.
    D. Omri knows it is all Gillon can afford.

3. What is special about the key Omri finds to lock the cupboard?
    A. The key was to his grandfather's safe. Omri's mother wears it on a chain around her neck to keep it from getting lost.
    B. The key was to his great-grandfather's desk. Omri's mother had worn it around her neck until the ribbon broke, and she almost lost it.
    C. The key was to his grandmother's jewel box. Omri's mother wears it on a ribbon around her neck to keep it safe.
    D. The key was to his great-grandmother's jewel box. Omri's mother had worn it around her neck until the ribbon broke, and she almost lost it.

4. When Omri discovers the live Indian in the cupboard why does he decide to keep it a secret?
    A. He doesn't want his mother to take the key away.
    B. He know he is just dreaming.
    C. Omri is afraid his family will laugh and accuse him of telling lies.
    D. The Indian told him to keep it a secret.

5. What is Omri's reaction when the Indian threatens to kill Omri if he touches the Indian?
    A. Omri throws the Indian back into the cupboard and locks the door.
    B. Omri pins the Indian down with his finger.
    C. Even though there is a vast difference in their sizes and strengths, Omri respects the Indian and is afraid.
    D. Omri yells at the Indian that he is not afraid and the Indian hides in the cupboard.

6. After Omri drops several tantalizing hints to Patrick about Little Bear, what is Patrick's reaction?
    A. Patrick tells Omri that it is not funny to tease your friends.
    B. Patrick asks Omri if he is being sarcastic and then he tells Omri he doesn't believe him.
    C. Patrick asks if he can see Little Bear.
    D. Patrick calls Omri a liar and never speaks to him again.

7. Before going to breakfast Omri locks the Indian back in the cupboard and does not return to it until after school. What does Omri discover when he opens the cupboard?
    A. He finds an entire tribe of Indians in the cupboard.
    B. He doesn't find anything. The Indian is gone.
    C. He finds the Indian lying on the floor of the cupboard, and he is plastic again.
    D. He finds the Indian dead on the shelf in the cupboard.

8. What does Omri do when the Indian asks for food?
    A. Omri sneaks into the kitchen and gets the Indian corn, bread, and cheese to eat and Coke to drink.
    B. Omri tells his mother he is hungry and she fixes him a snack which he shares with the Indian.
    C. Omri gives the Indian candy he had in his pocket.
    D. Omri sneaks into the kitchen and cooks bacon and eggs for the Indian.

9. How does the Indian introduce himself?
    A. He points at himself proudly and says, "Big Bear. Iroquois brave. Son of chief."
    B. He points at himself proudly and says, "Little Bear. Iroquois brave. Son of chief."
    C. He points at himself proudly and says, "Big Bear. Iroquois chief."
    D. He points at himself proudly and says, "Little Bear. Iroquois chief."

10. Where does Little Bear sleep during his first night with Omri?
    A. He is too afraid to sleep so he sits up all night.
    B. He sleeps in Omri's tennis shoe with a sock for a blanket.
    C. He sleeps in a toy truck with a kleenex for a blanket.
    D. He sleeps in a tepee made by Omri with a blanket cut from Omri's sweater.

Assignment #2
Chapters 3-5

1. Why does Omri consider turning Little Bear back into plastic?
    A. Little Bear threatens to kill Omri.
    B. He knows he will not be able to keep Little Bear a secret.
    C. After a discussion of war and scalping, Omri realizes that Little Bear is real, not a toy or an actor.
    D. After a discussion of war and scalping, Omri realizes that Little Bear is too dangerous.

2. What does Little Bear tell Omri when he asks if Little Bear has a wife?
    A. Little Bear tells Omri he never wanted to get married.
    B. Little Bear tells Omri that chief warriors are not allowed to marry.
    C. Little Bear tells Omri he is too young to be married.
    D. Little Bear tells Omri his wife is dead.

3. Why does Omri take Little Bear and his horse outside?
    A. Little Bear wants to look for European traders.
    B. Little Bear wants to go hunting.
    C. Little Bear wants to ride his horse on the ground, not on the carpet.
    D. Little Bear wants to explore his new surroundings and find a place to establish a village.

4. When Little Bear realizes all the dangers outside, what does he request from Omri?
    A. He asks for fire, food, and water.
    B. He asks for steel knives, spears, and cannons.
    C. He pleads for Omri to locate more Iroquois Indians to help him set up the new village.
    D. He asks Omri for Indian weapons: bow, arrows, and a club. He also asks for a gun.

5. Why does Omri bring the First World War soldier to life?
    A. Omri wants to give Little Bear some of the soldier's rations and tools.
    B. The soldier is a medical orderly and Omri needs a bandage the right size for Little Bear's leg.
    C. Omri thought it would be exciting for Little Bear to meet someone from another place and time.
    D. The soldier is a medical orderly and Omri wants to use his thermometer, iodine, and painkillers.

6. What does the soldier think of Omri?
    A. The soldier thinks Omri is a magician.
    B. The soldier thinks Omri is god.
    C. The soldier thinks Omri is a dream.
    D. The soldier thinks Omri is going to kill him.

7. What type of house does Little Bear want to build?
    A. He wants to build a wigwam.
    B. He wants to build a lodge.
    C. He wants to build a tepee.
    D. He wants to build a longhouse.

8. Why does Omri place a knight inside the cupboard?
    A. He wants to give Little Bear the knight's battle-ax.
    B. He wants to use parts of the knight's protective clothing for Little Bear's horse.
    C. He wants to give Little Bear the knight's longbow and shield.
    D. He wants the knight to protect Little Bear's home.

9. What elements together magically bring toys to life?
    A. The cupboard had to be opened with Omri's great-grandmother's key and the toys had to be made of metal.
    B. The toys had to be made of plastic and placed upside down in the cupboard.
    C. The toys had to be made of plastic and appear realistic to come alive.
    D. The toys must be made of plastic and the cupboard must be locked with Omri's great-grandmother's key.

Assignment #3
Chapters 6-7

1. Why does Omri use part of his lunch money to buy the Indian chief?
    A. He buys the Indian chief because he wants Little Bear and the chief to battle.
    B. He buys the Indian chief so Little Bear will not forget his culture.
    C. He buys the Indian chief for the bow and arrows to give to Little Bear.
    D. He buys the Indian chief so Little Bear will have a friend his own size.

2. What shocks Omri about the Indian chief?
    A. When Omri opens the cupboard, the Indian chief is still plastic.
    B. The Indian chief speaks perfect English and helps translate what Little Bear is saying.
    C. The Indian chief is hostile and orders Little Bear to attack Omri.
    D. The Indian chief dies right after Omri brings him to life.

3. What has Omri done to make his father angry?
    A. Omri has taken a seed tray from his father's greenhouse and cut bark off the birch tree.
    B. Omri has taken some steak from the refrigerator.
    C. Omri has lied to his mother about cleaning his room.
    D. Omri has taken a water bucket and potting soil from his father's greenhouse.

4. Why does Omri tell Patrick about Little Bear?
    A. Since Patrick enjoys history, Omri wants to get some advice from him about Iroquois Indians.
    B. Omri feels that he can trust Patrick with his secret.
    C. Omri needs someone to help him manage all the responsibilities.
    D. Omri doesn't want to lose Patrick's friendship. He also wants to show someone else his Indian.

5. Omri runs into Patrick when he comes out of the hardware store. What does Patrick have for Omri?
    A. Patrick has a book about Iroquois Indians.
    B. Patrick has a plastic Indian woman.
    C. Patrick has some of his little sister's doll clothes to give to Little Bear.
    D. Patrick has a plastic cowboy on a horse.

6. Why is Omri upset that his brothers are in his room when he returns from the hardware store?
    A. Omri's brothers' rat has been chewing on Little Bear's longhouse.
    B. Omri sees them playing with Little Bear and is afraid they will tell someone.
    C. Omri is not allowed to go in their room, so he doesn't want to let them in his.
    D. Omri is afraid the boys will discover Little Bear or that the rat will injure him.

7. What is Patrick's reaction when he sees Little Bear for the first time?
    A. Patrick screams. Omri puts his hand over Patrick's mouth and holds him down to stop him from running out of the room.
    B. Patrick swallows, his eyes seem in danger of popping out of his head, and he doesn't speak when Little Bear speaks to him.
    C. Patrick starts jumping around the room in excitement and begs Omri to try putting more figures into the cupboard.
    D. Patrick touches Little Bear's hand, softly says hello to him, and then faints.

8. Which of the following does NOT worry Omri?
    A. He thinks his mother overheard him talking to Little Bear.
    B. He doesn't want to lose Patrick's friendship.
    C. He wants Little Bear to be safe.
    D. He doesn't want anyone else to find out about Little Bear.

Assignment #4
Chapters 8-9

1. What spoils Little Bear's steak dinner?
   A. Little Bear is practicing using the bow and arrow Omri gave him, and he forgets to watch the fire. The fire gets out of hand, consumes the steak, and leaves a burn mark on Omri's table.
   B. Omri's mother enters the room as Little Bear is cooking the steak. Omri quickly throws a blanket over Little Bear to hide him, and the blanket smothers the fire.
   C. Omri and Patrick argue and Omri shoves Patrick causing him to tip the plate, spilling the fire on the carpet and making the meat roll under Omri's foot.
   D. Gillon's rat gets loose again and tries to eat Little Bear. Little Bear throws his steak to distract the rat and hides in his longhouse.

2. What does Patrick do when Omri leaves his room to get Little Bear something else for his dinner?
   A. Patrick puts Little Bear back in the cupboard.
   B. Patrick puts the plastic cowboy and his horse in the cupboard.
   C. Patrick asks Little Bear about his life as an Indian.
   D. Patrick hides the key to the cupboard in his backpack.

3. What is Omri afraid will happen if Little Bear and the cowboy meet?
   A. Omri is afraid they will band together and try to escape.
   B. Omri is afraid they will kill each other.
   C. Omri is afraid they will be scared of one another.
   D. Omri is afraid they will become friends and Little Bear won't want to talk to him (Omri) anymore.

4. Patrick agrees to let Omri take care of his cowboy the first night, but what does he threaten to do if Omri puts the cowboy back in the cupboard or does not bring him to school the next day?
   A. Patrick threatens to put a plastic dinosaur in the cupboard.
   B. Patrick threatens to throw the cupboard key in the dumpster.
   C. Patrick threatens to kill Little Bear.
   D. Patrick threatens to tell about Little Bear and the cowboy.

5. Where does Omri decide to keep the cowboy and his horse the first night?
   A. Omri puts them on the top of his bookshelf where they cannot possibly jump down.
   B. Omri cleans out the dressing-up crate and puts the cowboy and his horse in there.
   C. Omri puts them in the bathtub.
   D. Omri empties his sock drawer and puts the cowboy and his horse in it.

6. What does the cowboy do that upsets Omri?
    A. The cowboy cries, and Omri does not know what to do.
    B. The cowboy beats his horse.
    C. The cowboy starts screaming, and Omri is afraid his family will hear.
    D. The cowboy tries to shoot Little Bear.

7. What does Omri have to do to get Little Bear to dance?
    A. Omri must get Little Bear a new gun.
    B. Omri must turn Boone back into plastic.
    C. Omri must feed him.
    D. Omri must get Little Bear a wife.

8. What sound wakes Omri up at dawn?
    A. He hears the television turn on.
    B. He hears his mother coming upstairs.
    C. He hears shots.
    D. He hears his brothers' screams.

9. How does the cowboy escape from the crate?
    A. The cowboy pushes out (or perhaps the horse kicks) a knot in the wood, leaving an oval-shaped hole like an arched doorway.
    B. He climbs through an opening at the top of the crate.
    C. He shoots a hole through the side of the crate.
    D. He uses a rope to climb up the side of the crate.

10. How does Omri convince Little Bear not to kill the cowboy?
    A. Omri tells Little Bear he will take away Little Bear's horse if he kills the cowboy.
    B. Omri tells Little Bear he will not get him a wife if he kills the cowboy.
    C. Omri tells Little Bear he will take him to school.
    D. Omri convinces Little Bear that the cowboy is an Englishman.

11. What is Boone's nickname? Why?
    A. Boone's nickname is Slim because of his appearance.
    B. Boone's nickname is Smiley because he always has a goofy smile on his face.
    C. Boone's nickname is Boohoo because he cries so easily.
    D. Boone's nickname is Bronco because he can tame crazy horses.

Assignment #5
Chapters 10-12

1. How does Omri get Boone to eat breakfast with Little Bear?
    A. Omri promises Boone that food will stop him from having hallucy-nations.
    B. Omri threatens to tell Little Bear Boone's nickname.
    C. Omri takes Little Bear's bow and arrows and gives them to Boone.
    D. Omri cooks Boone's favorite foods over a campfire.

2. After breakfast Boone and Little Bear fight. How does Omri stop the fight?
    A. Omri picks them up in his hands and tells them fighting is wrong.
    B. Omri pins both men down with his finger and tells them the fight is a draw.
    C. Omri dumps a glass of water on them.
    D. Omri blows a whistle right next to them, startling them and making them stop.

3. Why does Omri bring Boone and Little Bear an egg cup filled with hot water?
    A. He wants them to be able to brush their teeth.
    B. He wants them to use it to clean their clothes.
    C. He is angry with them about the fight and tells them to start cooking their own food.
    D. He wants them to bathe before he takes them to school.

4. What does Omri tell Boone and Little Bear will happen if they are seen at school?
    A. Omri tells them they could be taken by the government and studied by scientists.
    B. Omri tells them the other children will be scared and try to smash them.
    C. Omri tells them they will be taken by the teacher and the whole school will find out about them.
    D. Omri tells them they could be taken away from Omri and then they would not be able to get back to their own time.

5. What happens outside the school when Omri gives Boone to Patrick?
    A. A girl sees it and tells the other kids. Soon Omri and Patrick are surrounded and they must quickly barge through the pack of children.
    B. Patrick wants to show the other students his amazing cowboy, and he calls everyone to come over to him.
    C. Boone throws a fit because he doesn't trust Patrick and wants Omri to continue protecting him.
    D. Boone slips out of Patrick's hand and falls on the sidewalk. His leg is broken, and the boys don't know how to help him.

6. What makes Omri let out a short yelp in the main hall?
    A. Little Bear jabs Omri with his knife.
    B. Boone and Little Bear start fighting again.
    C. He is worried Patrick is hurting Boone.
    D. He sees Mr. Johnson angrily walking toward him.

7. At lunch Omri gives Boone and Little Bear to Patrick. What does Omri tell Patrick he will do if anything happens to Little Bear?
    A. Omri says, "If you let anything happen to Little Bear, I will bash you so hard your teeth will fall out."
    B. Omri says, "If you let anything happen to Little Bear, you will be sorry you ever put Boone in that cupboard."
    C. Omri says, "If you let anything happen to Little Bear, I will probably never talk to you again."
    D. Omri says, "If you let anything happen to Little Bear, I don't ever want to see your face again."

8. Why do Patrick and Omri get sent to Mr. Johnson, the headmaster's office?
    A. A teacher sees the commotion outside the school and thinks Patrick and Omri are responsible for it.
    B. Patrick and Omri start fighting outside the school.
    C. Patrick is late for class, and Omri is sent to Mr. Johnson for talking in class.
    D. The boys seemed distracted and unusual all day, and Mr. Johnson is concerned about them.

9. Why does Omri knock Patrick down, sit on his chest, and pin Patrick's hands to the ground in Mr. Johnson's office?
    A. Omri doesn't want Patrick to show Boone and Little Bear to Mr. Johnson.
    B. Omri notices Little Bear and Boone crawling out of Patrick's pocket.
    C. Omri is trying to rescue Boone and Little Bear.
    D. Omri is trying to throw Mr. Johnson off track.

10. What happens after Mr. Johnson throws Omri out of his office?
    A. Omri runs straight home.
    B. Patrick tells Mr. Johnson that Omri is crazy and thinks his toys can come to life.
    C. Patrick shows Little Bear to Mr. Johnson.
    D. Mr. Johnson gives Patrick detention for causing trouble.

Assignment #6
Chapters 13-14

1. What condition are Little Bear and Boone in when Patrick gives them back to Omri in the bathroom?
    A. Little Bear and Boone are terrified, clinging to each other. Even Little Bear is hiding his face.
    B. Little Bear and Boone are angry and covered with cuts and scrapes; they have been fighting again.
    C. Little Bear and Boone are confused. They heard all the commotion but couldn't tell what everyone was talking about.
    D. Little Bear and Boone are cramped and irritable from staying still all day.

2. Why doesn't Omri give Boone and Little Bear back to Patrick?
    A. Boone and Little Bear say they would prefer to stay with Omri.
    B. Omri tells Patrick they are not safe with him. He says Patrick uses them and "you can't use people."
    C. Omri knows that Mr. Johnson will try to get Boone and Little Bear from Patrick, so he must keep them as far from Patrick as possible.
    D. Omri decides he doesn't need Patrick's help anymore and doesn't want to share Little Bear and Boone with him.

3. During art class, what does Omri learn about Boone?
    A. Art was Boone's best subject when he was in school, and he can draw very well.
    B. Boone cannot tell the difference between the paints, so he must be colorblind.
    C. Boone is allergic to the chemicals in modern paper. He begins to break out in a rash.
    D. Boone took art classes in school and hated them.

4. Why does Omri burst out laughing when he leaves his art class?
    A. He realizes how glad he is that Boone is there, even though he had always been mad that Patrick brought him to life.
    B. Boone and Little Bear begin moving around in Omri's backpack and it tickles.
    C. He had fooled his art teacher by pretending Boone's drawing is his own original creation.
    D. He is thrilled that he made it through the day without losing Boone and Little Bear.

5. Who stands up for Omri when Mr. Yapp accuses him of stealing?
    A. Patrick stands up for Omri.
    B. Gillon stands up for Omri.
    C. Nobody. Omri has no proof that he didn't steal.
    D. Mr. Johnson stands up for Omri.

6. Why does Adiel take the cupboard from Omri's room?
   A. Adiel needs something to put his football trophies in. Since the cupboard is empty, he assumes Omri is not using it.
   B. Adiel has always liked the cupboard and thinks he deserves it just as much as Omri does.
   C. Adiel got detention for not having his football shorts. He thinks Omri has taken them, so he takes the cupboard to teach Omri a lesson.
   D. Adiel hears a rumor at school that Omri has a magical cupboard. He wants to see if the rumor is true.

7. When Omri gets the cupboard back, why is it's magic gone?
   A. There is a large crack on the side.
   B. One of the doors won't close properly.
   C. The key is missing.
   D. Little Bear and Boone have been outside the cupboard for too long. The magic has been used up.

8. What happens to Boone while he and Little Bear are watching a Western on TV?
   A. Angered by the killing of Indians in the Western TV show, Little Bear shoots Boone with an arrow.
   B. Boone falls asleep and slips between the couch cushions. Omri and Patrick can't find him.
   C. Patrick gets up to get a drink and when he comes back he accidentally sits on Boone.
   D. Boone sees the cowboys on TV and it reminds him of his old life. He begins to feel very homesick.

9. Who removes the arrow from Boone's chest?
   A. Omri removes the arrow using his mother's tweezers.
   B. Boone pulls the arrow out himself.
   C. Little Bear removes the arrow because Omri and Patrick are too big to do it safely.
   D. Patrick removes the arrow with his teeth.

10. What happens to Little Bear's headdress?
    A. Little Bear throws it on the ground and jumps on it, breaking all the feathers.
    B. Gillon's rat gets loose again and eats it.
    C. Little Bear gives it to Boone as an apology for shooting him with the arrow.
    D. Boone steals it to get back at Little Bear.

Assignment #7
Chapters 15-16

1. Why does Omri move the seed box and Boone's bed up off the floor?
    A. Gillon's rat is loose, and Omri is afraid for Boone and Little Bear.
    B. Omri wants to talk to Boone and Little Bear while he falls asleep, and he can't hear them on the floor.
    C. Boone and Little Bear say it's too cold down by the floor.
    D. Omri thinks of them as equals now, and says they deserve a higher spot.

2. Why does Omri put Little Bear under the floor in his bedroom?
    A. Omri has to leave Little Bear in his room when he leaves the house. He thinks under the floor is the only place where his brothers will not look.
    B. Omri drops a twenty dollar bill between the floorboards and needs Little Bear to reach it.
    C. Omri realizes the missing key must have fallen through the floor, and he asks Little Bear to find it.
    D. Omri puts Little Bear in time out for being rude to Boone.

3. Why does Patrick ask if Little Bear has his bow and arrows with him under the floor?
    A. Patrick wants to know if Little Bear can defend himself from cockroaches.
    B. Patrick is afraid Little Bear will lose his bow and arrows while he is looking for the key.
    C. Patrick thinks the bow and arrow are probably weighing Little Bear down and offers to take them for him.
    D. Patrick wants to know if Little Bear can defend himself from Gillon's rat.

4. Why is Omri so worried about Little Bear and Gillon's rat?
    A. Omri knows the rat has not been fed in several days.
    B. Omri knows Little Bear is not as strong as the rat.
    C. Omri knows that rats have good vision in the dark.
    D. Omri knows he will never forgive himself if Little Bear is killed.

5. When Little Bear returns with the key what does Omri do?
    A. Omri immediately brings Tommy (the medical orderly) back to life to help Boone.
    B. Omri prepares a big feast to thank Little Bear.
    C. Omri jumps up and down with excitement.
    D. Omri immediately puts the Indian woman in the cupboard.

6. What had not yet been discovered in Tommy's time?
    A. Aspirin had not been discovered.
    B. The microscope had not been discovered.
    C. X-rays had not been discovered.
    D. Penicillin had not been discovered.

7. Why does Little Bear get angry when Boone finds out it was Little Bear who shot him?
    A. Little Bear gets angry because Boone threatens to fight him if anything like that happens again.
    B. Little Bear gets angry because Boone doesn't seem to be any more afraid of him now.
    C. Little Bear gets angry because Boone just laughs and tells Little Bear to work on his aim.
    D. Little Bear gets angry because Boone is more concerned with what happened in the TV show between the settlers and the Indians.

8. Why does Little Bear give Omri his belt made of white beads?
    A. He gives Omri the belt as payment for his new wife.
    B. He gives Omri the belt to give to Boone.
    C. He gives Omri the belt as a peace offering.
    D. He gives Omri the belt to bring to art class.

9. What makes Omri realize he needs to send Little Bear, his wife, and Boone back to their own time?
    A. Boone becomes very depressed and quiet, and Omri knows it's because he misses being a real cowboy.
    B. Little Bear begins to tell his wife all the wonderful and exciting stories of his life as an Indian.
    C. Omri feels he can no longer keep such a big secret from his family.
    D. When Little Bear tells Omri what he wants for his wedding, Omri realizes Little Bear will be happier in his own time.

10. After Omri puts Little Bear, his wife, and Boone in the cupboard, why does Little Bear ask for Omri's hand?

    A. Little Bear puts a feather in Omri's hand so that he will never forget Little Bear.
    B. Before going back to his own time Little Bear wants to thank Omri again for getting him a wife.
    C. Before going back to his own time Little Bear wants to make Omri his blood brother.
    D. Little Bear wants to thank Omri for protecting him, but he doesn't know the words to say. He shakes Omri's hand and Omri understands.

11. What does Omri's mother tell him she will do with the key when he asks her to keep it for him?

    A. She tells him that it will be in her jewelry box if he ever needs it.
    B. She tells him she will put it in a safe so that he cannot get to it unless he is really sure he wants it.
    C. She tells him that it is meant to be with the cupboard.
    D. She tells him she will get a chain and wear it like she always meant to.

ANSWER KEY: STUDY QUESTIONS *The Indian in the Cupboard*

	1	2	3	4	5	6	7
1	C	C	C	C	B	A	A
2	B	D	D	B	B	B	C
3	D	C	A	B	D	A	D
4	C	D	D	D	D	C	D
5	C	B	D	B	A	A	A
6	B	C	D	A	A	C	D
7	C	D	B	D	A	C	D
8	A	A	A	C	C	A	A
9	B	D		A	A	C	D
10	D			B	C	A	C
11				C			D

VOCABULARY WORKSHEETS

VOCABULARY ASSIGNMENT #1 *The Indian in the Cupboard*

Part I: Using Prior Knowledge and Contextual Clues

Below are the sentences in which the vocabulary words appear in the text. Read the sentence. Use any clues you can find in the sentence combined with your prior knowledge, and write what you think the underlined words mean on the lines provided.

1. He stood pressed against the inside wall of the cupboard, clutching his knife, rigid with terror, but <u>defiant</u>.

   _____

2. The first <u>coherent</u> thought that came into Omri's mind as he began to get over the shock was, "I must call the others!"

   _____

3. He wore a kind of <u>bandolier</u> across his chest and his belt seemed to be made of several strands of some shiny white beads.

   _____

4. It was the only way he would ever be able to see and appreciate the <u>intricate</u> details of the Indian's clothes.

   _____

5. <u>Unwarily</u>, Omri replied, "Oh I don't think he can *write* English, he can only just speak"--

   _____

6. Omri knelt there, appalled- too <u>appalled</u> to move.

   _____

7. "What is it, Omri? Tell me," <u>coaxed</u> his mother.

   _____

8. "Tepee!" the Indian shouted, "I no live tepee. I live <u>longhouse</u>!"

   _____

9. He put it on the shelf beside the Indian, who looked at it with the utmost <u>scorn</u>.

   _____

The Indian in the Cupboard Vocabulary Worksheet Assignment #1 Continued

Part II: Determining the Meaning -- Match the vocabulary words to their dictionary definitions.

____ 1.   DEFIANT   A.   A kind of belt worn over one shoulder and across the chest

____ 2.   COHERENT   B.   A long, bark-covered dwelling place built by some Native North American peoples, especially the Iroquois

____ 3.   BANDOLIER   C.   Containing many details or small parts that are skillfully made

____ 4.   INTRICATE   D.   Tending to confront and challenge

____ 5.   UNWARILY   E.   Not cautiously

____ 6.   APPALLED   F.   Shocked

____ 7.   COAXED   G.   Logical

____ 8.   LONGHOUSE   H.   A feeling of dislike

____ 9.   SCORN   I.   Persuaded gently

VOCABULARY ASSIGNMENT #2 *The Indian in the Cupboard*

Part I: Using Prior Knowledge and Contextual Clues
Below are the sentences in which the vocabulary words appear in the text. Read the sentence. Use any clues you can find in the sentence combined with your prior knowledge, and write what you think the underlined words mean on the lines provided.

1. The Indian folded his arms uncompromisingly across his chest.

   _____

2. The Indian rose lithely to his feet and jumped off onto the gray carpet.

   _____

3. Scalps? Omri swallowed. "How many?"

   _____

4. Down in the kitchen he ransacked his mother's store cupboard for a tin of meat.

   _____

5. Little Bear was clearly reluctant to return to the house, but he had the sense to realize he couldn't cope outside by himself.

   _____

6. Full of foreboding, Omri bent down and peered into the box.

   _____

7. By the time he got back to his own room, the soldier was kneeling at Little Bear's feet, applying a neat tourniquet to the top of his leg.

   _____

8. Regretfully, Omri shut and locked the door.

   _____

The Indian in the Cupboard Vocabulary Worksheet Assignment #2 Continued

Part II: Determining the Meaning -- Match the vocabulary words to their dictionary definitions.

____ 1. UNCOMPROMISINGLY   A. The skin and hair covering the skulls of enemies; cut off as trophies

____ 2. LITHELY   B. Unwilling to back down

____ 3. SCALPS   C. Searched thoroughly but handled carelessly

____ 4. RANSACKED   D. A tight band applied around an arm or a leg to stop bleeding

____ 5. RELUCTANT   E. A feeling that something bad is going to happen

____ 6. FOREBODING   F. Bending easily

____ 7. TOURNIQUET   G. Hesitant

____ 8. REGRETFULLY   H. Remorsefully

VOCABULARY ASSIGNMENT #3 *The Indian in the Cupboard*

Part I: Using Prior Knowledge and Contextual Clues

    Below are the sentences in which the vocabulary words appear in the text. Read the sentence. Use any clues you can find in the sentence combined with your prior knowledge, and write what you think the underlined words mean on the lines provided.

1. They had indeed lived in longhouses, not tepees, and their main foods had been <u>maize</u> and squash (whatever they were) and beans.

   _____

2. "You can buy them for a few <u>pence</u> in Yapp's."

   _____

3. "I wish you'd stop this stupid business," he said <u>peevishly</u>, "going on as if it weren't a joke."

   _____

4. He realized at once that his seed tray, as a seed tray, was lost to him forever and that it was no use <u>hectoring</u> Omri about it.

   _____

5. Omri was <u>galvanized</u> into action.

   _____

6. He gazed up <u>imperiously</u> at Patrick, who gazed back in wonder.

   _____

7. "Omri's friend, Little Bear's friend," said Little Bear <u>magnanimously</u>.

   _____

8. An <u>incredulous</u> grin spread over Patrick's face.

   _____

9. He'd had a wonderful idea for a <u>spit</u> to cook it on.

   _____

The Indian in the Cupboard Vocabulary Worksheet Assignment #3 Continued

Part II: Determining the Meaning -- Match the vocabulary words to their dictionary definitions.

____ 1.	MAIZE	A.	Nobly
____ 2.	PENCE	B.	A thin rod or bar on which meat is pierced for broiling or roasting over a fire
____ 3.	PEEVISHLY	C.	Speaking in a domineering tone
____ 4.	HECTORING	D.	Unbelieving
____ 5.	GALVANIZED	E.	Corn
____ 6.	IMPERIOUSLY	F.	Plural of penny
____ 7.	MAGNANIMOUSLY	G.	Domineeringly
____ 8.	INCREDULOUS	H.	Stimulated into great activity
____ 9.	SPIT	I.	Irritably

VOCABULARY ASSIGNMENT #4 *The Indian in the Cupboard*

Part I: Using Prior Knowledge and Contextual Clues

Below are the sentences in which the vocabulary words appear in the text. Read the sentence. Use any clues you can find in the sentence combined with your prior knowledge, and write what you think the underlined words mean on the lines provided.

1. Omri gaped at him.

   _____

2. Patrick looked mulish. "It was your fault. You should have let me put something in the cupboard."

   _____

3. There was a petrified moment when he couldn't move.

   _____

4. He ate ravenously for a few moments and then said, "Not want?"

   _____

5. "To school!" cried Omri aghast. "I'm not bringing Little Bear to school!"

   _____

6. The pony was tethered to his post on a long rope.

   _____

7. This infuriated the little man, who, forgetting his fear, stood up in his stirrups and shouted, "Tarnation take ya, ya, red varmint!..."

   _____

8. "No-" Omri began. Then he changed his tactics.

   _____

9. "You shore ain't no reg'lar hallucy-nation," he said. "I'm obliged to ya."

   _____

The Indian in the Cupboard Vocabulary Worksheet Assignment #4 Continued

Part II: Determining the Meaning -- Match the vocabulary words to their dictionary definitions.

____ 1.   GAPED A.   A course of action to achieve short-term gains

____ 2.   MULISH B.   Tied with a rope or chain

____ 3.   PETRIFIED C.   Unwilling to cooperate or listen to suggestions

____ 4.   RAVENOUSLY D.   Enraged

____ 5.   AGHAST E.   Indebted to do something for someone

____ 6.   TETHERED F.   Immobile with fear

____ 7.   INFURIATED G.   Overcome with shock

____ 8.   TACTICS H.   Stared in open-mouthed surprise

____ 9.   OBLIGED I.   Hungrily

VOCABULARY ASSIGNMENT #5 *The Indian in the Cupboard*

Part I: Using Prior Knowledge and Contextual Clues

Below are the sentences in which the vocabulary words appear in the text. Read the sentence. Use any clues you can find in the sentence combined with your prior knowledge, and write what you think the underlined words mean on the lines provided.

1. "All the best cooks are men," he <u>retorted</u>.

   _____

2. "Oh knock it off, Little Bear! Have a <u>truce</u> for breakfast, otherwise you won't get any."

   _____

3. He'd taken off the little saddle, the <u>bridle</u> was still on.

   _____

4. Omri had never arrived at school with more <u>apprehension</u> in his heart, not even on spelling-test days.

   _____

5. Once he had taken a white mouse to school in his blazer pocket. He'd planned to do all sorts of <u>fiendish</u> things with it...

   _____

6. "What've you got there then, what did he give you?" she asked in her <u>raucous</u> voice like a crow's.

   _____

7. There were teachers all over the place, and any kind of fighting or taunting, above a sly pinch or a <u>snide</u> whisper, was out.

   _____

8. Omri held his <u>persecutor</u> at eye level and shook him violently, the way you shake a bottle of medicine.

   _____

The Indian in the Cupboard Vocabulary Worksheet Assignment #5 Continued

Part II: Determining the Meaning -- Match the vocabulary words to their dictionary definitions.

____ 1. RETORTED   A. Oppressor; tyrant

____ 2. TRUCE   B. Sarcastic

____ 3. BRIDLE   C. A feeling of anxiety or fear that something bad is going to occur

____ 4. APPREHENSION   D. Loud and hoarse or unpleasant-sounding

____ 5. FIENDISH   E. A set of leather straps fitted to a horse's head that includes the bit and the reins

____ 6. RAUCOUS   F. Replied in quick response to something someone has said

____ 7. SNIDE   G. An agreed break in any type of dispute or feud

____ 8. PERSECUTOR   H. Devilish

VOCABULARY ASSIGNMENT #6 *The Indian in the Cupboard*

Part I: Using Prior Knowledge and Contextual Clues
    Below are the sentences in which the vocabulary words appear in the text. Read the sentence. Use any clues you can find in the sentence combined with your prior knowledge, and write what you think the underlined words mean on the lines provided.

1. Mrs. Hunt was obviously <u>flummoxed</u>.

   _____

2. It was a prairie landscape, with hills and cacti and a few tufts of <u>sagebrush</u>.

   _____

3. ...the drawing was <u>minute</u>, perfect in its detailing but smaller than any human hand could have possibly have made it.

   _____

4. Her face was not quite as stunned as Mr. Johnson's had been, but it was an absolute picture of <u>bafflement</u>.

   _____

5. Underneath the heaps were all the <u>myriad</u> little oddments that were small enough to filter through the bigger things--marbles, wheels of Matchbox cars, bits of Lego, small tools, parachute men, cards, and so on and so on,....

   _____

6. Omri was in <u>despair</u>.

   _____

7. Little Bear stopped chewing his chocolate the moment he saw her and gazed in <u>rapture</u>.

   _____

8. First came a film about animals, which absolutely <u>transfixed</u> both the little men.

   _____

9. Omri could sense Little Bear was getting <u>restive</u> and tense.

   _____

The Indian in the Cupboard Vocabulary Worksheet Assignment #6 Continued

Part II: Determining the Meaning -- Match the vocabulary words to their dictionary definitions.

____ 1. FLUMMOXED   A. Having little patience and on the verge of resisting control

____ 2. SAGEBRUSH   B. A feeling of hopelessness

____ 3. MINUTE   C. Bewilderment

____ 4. BAFFLEMENT   D. Numerous

____ 5. MYRIAD   E. A euphoric state in which somebody is overwhelmed by happiness and unaware of anything else

____ 6. DESPAIR   F. Made motionless

____ 7. RAPTURE   G. Extremely small

____ 8. TRANSFIXED   H. A bushy plant native to dry regions of North America with silvery wedge-shaped leaves and clusters of small white flowers

____ 9. RESTIVE   I. Perplexed

VOCABULARY ASSIGNMENT #7 *The Indian in the Cupboard*

Part I: Using Prior Knowledge and Contextual Clues
    Below are the sentences in which the vocabulary words appear in the text. Read the sentence. Use any clues you can find in the sentence combined with your prior knowledge, and write what you think the underlined words mean on the lines provided.

1. The <u>perils</u> that a rat presented to his little men simply turned his blood cold.

   _____

2. Patrick gazed at him in admiration, but also in <u>dismay</u>.

   _____

3. The rest were nailed down to the <u>joists</u> underneath.

   _____

4. Little Bear, a tiny, <u>vulnerable</u> figure, strode off through the dust into the darkness under the floor.

   _____

5. What else but a rat, gnawing away all day? A rat at this moment out on his night prowl, a hungry rat who hadn't eaten for twenty-four hours-- a pink-eyed, needle-toothed, <u>omnivorous</u>, giant rat?

   _____

6. "Could do with a blood <u>transfusion</u> really. I'll have to have this bandage off, and look at his wound...."

   _____

7. "We need penicillin for him," said Patrick, who had once had a bad cut on his foot that had turned <u>septic</u>.

   _____

8. He even pretended to have a <u>relapse</u>.

   _____

9. Boone looked at it in a <u>bemused</u> way and said, "Gee whiz. We done it! I'm part Injun!"

   _____

The Indian in the Cupboard Vocabulary Worksheet Assignment #7 Continued

Part II: Determining the Meaning -- Match the vocabulary words to their dictionary definitions.

____ 1.   PERILS   A.   Open to physical danger or harm

____ 2.   DISMAY   B.   Sources of potential harm

____ 3.   JOISTS   C.   Eating any kind of food, including both plants and animals

____ 4.   VULNERABLE   D.   Full of pus

____ 5.   OMNIVOROUS   E.   The transfer of blood into the bloodstream of somebody who has lost blood

____ 6.   TRANSFUSION   F.   To fall ill again after seeming to have made a recovery

____ 7.   SEPTIC   G.   Floor, roof, or ceiling supports

____ 8.   RELAPSE   H.   To dishearten, alarm, cause loss of courage

____ 9.   BEMUSED   I.   Puzzled

VOCABULARY ANSWER KEY - *The Indian in the Cupboard*

	1	2	3	4	5	6	7
1	D	B	E	H	F	I	B
2	G	F	F	C	G	H	H
3	A	A	I	F	E	G	G
4	C	C	C	I	C	C	A
5	E	G	H	G	H	D	C
6	F	E	G	B	D	B	E
7	I	D	A	D	B	E	D
8	B	H	D	A	A	F	F
9	H		B	E		A	I

DAILY LESSONS

LESSON ONE

Objectives
    1. To introduce *The Indian in the Cupboard* unit
    2. To discuss the meaning of friendship
    3. To preview the study questions and vocabulary for Chapters 1-2
    4. To read Chapters 1-2

Activity #1
Brainstorm about the term "friendship" by having students list the qualities they look for in a friend. Discuss what qualities are most important and why. Elaborate on the concept of "best friend" by discussing how a best friend differs from a regular friend or an acquaintance. Inquire about the benefits of having friends who are different from you. Can friendship change over time? Can you be mad at or jealous of a friend?

Share the following quote by Henry David Thoreau: "The language of friendship is not words but meanings." Discuss what the quotation implies about the nature of friendship.

Transition: Tell students the book they are going to read is about a boy, Omri, and the life-changing decisions he must make regarding friendship, trust, and responsibility for one's actions.

Activity #2
Distribute the materials students will use in this unit. Explain in detail how students are to use these materials.

Study Guides
Students should read the study guide questions for each reading assignment prior to beginning the reading assignment to get a feeling for what events and ideas are important in the section they are about to read. After reading the section, students will (as a class or individually) answer the questions to review the important events and ideas from that section of the book. Students should keep the study guides as study materials for the unit test. **Read through the study questions for Chapters 1-2 orally as a class.**

Vocabulary
Prior to each reading assignment, students will do vocabulary work related to the section of the book they are about to read. Following the completion of the reading of the book, there will be a vocabulary review of all the words used in the vocabulary assignments. Students should keep their vocabulary work as study materials for the unit test. **Do the vocabulary worksheet for Chapters 1-2 with your class to show them how they will do the other vocabulary worksheets in this unit.**

Reading Assignment Sheet
You need to fill in the reading assignment sheet to let students know by when their reading has to be completed. You can either write the assignment sheet up on the side blackboard or bulletin board and leave it there for students to see each day, or you can make copies for each student to have. In either case, you should advise students to become very familiar with the reading assignments so they know what is expected of them.

Extra Activities Center
The Unit Resource Materials portion of this LitPlan contains suggestions for an extra library of related books and articles in your classroom as well as crossword and word search puzzles. Make an extra activities center in your room where you will keep these materials for students to use.

(Bring the books and articles in from the library and keep several copies of the puzzles on hand.) Explain to students that these materials are available for students to use when they finish reading assignments or other class work early.

Non-fiction Assignment Sheet
Explain to students that they each are to read at least one non-fiction piece from the in-class library at some time during the unit. Students will fill out a Non-fiction Assignment Sheet after completing the reading to help you (the teacher) evaluate their reading experiences and to help the students think about and evaluate their own reading experiences.

Books
Each school has its own rules and regulations regarding student use of school books. Advise students of the procedures that are normal for your school. Preview the book. Look at the covers, front matter, and index. Glance through at some of the drawings.

Activity #3
Begin reading Chapters 1-2 together orally as a class. If class time runs out before the chapters are read, tell students to finish reading them prior to the next class.

LESSON TWO

Objectives
1. To review the main events and ideas of Chapters 1-2
2. To introduce Legends, Myths, and Folktales

Activity #1
Give students a few minutes to formulate answers to the study guide questions from Chapters 1-2 then discuss the answers to the questions in detail. Write the answers on the board so students can have the correct answers for study purposes.

NOTE: It is good practice in public speaking and leadership skills for individual students to take charge of leading the discussions of the study questions. Perhaps a different student could go to the front of the class and lead the discussion each day that the study questions are discussed in this unit. Of course, you should guide the discussion when appropriate and try to fill in any gaps students may leave. The study questions could really be handled in a number of different ways, including in small groups with group reports following. Occasionally you may want to use the multiple choice questions as quizzes to check students' reading comprehension. As a short review now and then, students could pair up for the first (or last, if you have time left at the end of a class period) few minutes of class to quiz each other from the study questions. Mix up the methods of reviewing the materials and checking comprehension throughout the unit so students don't get bored just answering the questions the same way each day. Variety in methods will also help address the different learning styles of your students.

From now on in this unit the directions will simply say, "Discuss the answers to the study questions as previously directed." You will choose the method of preparation and discussion each day based on what best suits you and your class.

Activity #2
Hold a short discussion on legends, myths, and folklore. Write down some of the different elements in legends, myths, and folktales. Have students name the legends, myths, and folktales they have heard.

Explain to the class that folktales from around the world often use familiar characteristics (called motifs). Identify common motifs (magic, supernatural powers, trickery, talking animals, etc.) in some of the folktales named by students. These stories have various functions such as to entertain, to explain something (natural phenomena, creation of the world, religious practices), or to teach a lesson.

Activity #3
Explain to students they will be doing a writing assignment in which they will be creating their own folktale. To prepare for this writing assignment they will read and report on a popular or famous folktale prior to beginning their own story.

Choose the folktales for your students to read or let them select their own. The Internet is a great source for locating a variety of folktales. Listed below are a few suggestions of both U.S. and Native American folklore:

Babe the Blue Ox
The Birth of Paul Bunyan
Heron and the Hummingbird
Three Billy Goats Gruff
The Trickster Tricked

John Henry
Ethan Allen
Pecos Bill Rides a Tornado
Davey Crockett

Divide your class into groups depending on the number of stories you have selected. Each group will be responsible for one story. Distribute copies of the stories to group members along with a project guide. Discuss the group project in detail.

GROUP PROJECT GUIDE *The Indian in the Cupboard*

Name of your story:_____

You have been given copies of a folktale.

1. Read the story out loud, taking turns reading and helping each other with any problem areas.

2. Write down the names of the main characters in the story:

NAME	NOTES ABOUT THE CHARACTER

Next to each character's name write a few words about that character

3. Write down a list of the main events of the story (in order).

4. What was the main problem in the story? How was it resolved?

GROUP PROJECT GUIDE *The Indian in the Cupboard* continued

5. What is the point of the story? Is there a lesson to learn?

6. What characteristics of myths, legends, or folktales does you story have?

LESSON THREE

<u>Objective</u>
    To practice public speaking skills

<u>Activity #1</u>
Have each group report to the class about its story. Each group member should report about one item on their project worksheets. After all groups have reported, ask students how the stories were alike and hold a brief discussion comparing (and contrasting) the stories.

Ask which story students liked best and why.

LESSON FOUR

Objectives
1. To preview the study questions and complete the vocabulary work for Chapters 3-5
2. To read Chapters 3-5
3. To evaluate students' oral reading

Activity #1
Give students time to preview the study questions and complete the vocabulary work for Chapters 3-5. Discuss and post the answers to the vocabulary worksheet so all students will have the correct answers for study purposes.

Activity #2
Have students read Chapters 3-5 orally so you can evaluate students' oral reading skills. You probably know the best way to choose readers in your class: pick students at random, ask for volunteers, or use whatever method works best with your group. If you have not completed an oral reading evaluation for your students this marking period, this would be a good opportunity to do so. An evaluation form has been included in this unit for your convenience.

ORAL READING EVALUATION - *Indian in the Cupboard*

Name _____ Class____ Date _____

SKILL	EXCELLENT	GOOD	AVERAGE	FAIR	POOR
Fluency	5	4	3	2	1
Clarity	5	4	3	2	1
Audibility	5	4	3	2	1
Pronunciation	5	4	3	2	1
_____	5	4	3	2	1
_____	5	4	3	2	1

Total ____ Grade

Comments:

LESSON FIVE

<u>Objectives</u>
1. To review the main events and ideas of Chapters 3-5
2. To practice writing to persuade
3. To evaluate students' writing skills

<u>Activity #1</u>
Discuss the answers to the study questions from Chapters 3-5 as previously directed.

<u>Activity #2</u>
In Chapter Three, Omri considers telling someone about Little Bear. While Omri decides if he wants to give up his secret, he realizes the enormity of his responsibility toward Little Bear. Open a discussion with students, asking them to list the pros and cons of Omri's sharing his secret. Write these on the board as a reference for students as they work on Writing Assignment #1.

<u>Activity #3</u>
Distribute Writing Assignment #1 and discuss the directions in detail. Tell students this writing assignment will be due at the end of the next class meeting.

WRITING ASSIGNMENT #1 *The Indian in the Cupboard*

PROMPT

In Chapter Three, Omri realizes Little Bear is not just a toy come to life, but a real person who somehow magically came out of the past. Omri thinks that maybe he ought to tell someone about Little Bear. While he is deciding if he wants to give up his secret, he realizes the enormity of his responsibility toward Little Bear. Should Omri tell someone about Little Bear?

Your assignment is to write a persuasive letter to Omri that will convince him to tell or not tell about Little Bear.

PREWRITING

Jot down notes regarding the following questions: Should Omri tell someone about Little Bear? Why or Why not? Who should Omri tell? Another child or an adult? Will he be able to care for Little Bear? What might happen to Little Bear if Omri doesn't tell? What might happen to Little Bear if he does tell? What will happen when Omri and Little Bear get older? What might happen to Omri if he keeps Little Bear to himself? Then fill out this chart of reason to (or not to) tell about Little Bear.

REASON TO TELL ABOUT LITTLE BEAR	REASONS NOT TO TELL ABOUT LITTLE BEAR

DRAFTING

Introduction

Topic sentence (Your opinion as to whether or not Omri should tell about Little Bear)

_____
_____
_____

Sentence 1_____
_____
_____

Sentence 2_____
_____
_____

Paragraph 2

Topic Sentence (one reason)_____

_____

_____

Sentence 2_____

_____

_____

Sentence 3_____

_____

_____

Paragraph 3

Topic Sentence (one reason)_____

_____

_____

Sentence 2_____

_____

_____

Sentence 3_____

_____

_____

Closing Paragraph

Topic Sentence)_____

_____

_____

Sentence 2_____

_____

_____

Sentence 3_____

_____

_____

PROOFREADING

As homework, read your work out loud. Reading aloud will help you hear what your eyes did not see. After reading aloud, double-check your grammar, spelling, organization, and the clarity of your ideas. If possible, put your paper aside for a short duration, then proofread it one more time.

WRITING EVALUATION FORM - *The Indian in the Cupboard*

Name _____ Date_____

Grade_____

Circle One For Each Item:

Grammar:	correct	errors noted on paper
Spelling:	correct	errors noted on paper
Punctuation:	correct	errors noted on paper
Legibility:	excellent	good fair poor
	excellent	good fair poor
	excellent	good fair poor

Strengths:

Weaknesses:

Comments/Suggestions:

LESSON SIX

<u>Objectives</u>
1. To preview the study questions and vocabulary for Chapters 6-7
2. To read Chapters 6-7
3. To allow students to complete Writing Assignment #1

<u>Activity #1</u>
Give students time to reread their persuasive letters and make any changes necessary. Collect this assignment prior to the end of the class.

<u>Activity #2</u>
Review the study questions and complete the vocabulary work for Chapters 6-7 together as a class.

<u>Activity #3</u>
Read Chapters 6-7. If you have completed the oral evaluations, students may read silently.

LESSON SEVEN

Objectives
1. To review the main events and ideas of Chapters 6-7
2. To distribute the guidelines for Writing Assignment #2
3. To demonstrate an understanding of the elements of folktales
4. To logically think through plot elements
5. To practice descriptive writing
6. To practice and demonstrate the ability to think creatively

Activity #1
Discuss the answers to the study questions from Chapters 6-7 as previously directed.

Activity #2
Distribute Writing Assignment # 2 and discuss the directions in detail. Tell students they will be writing a folktale which will be due at the end of this unit.

Give students the remaining class time to start this assignment. Answer any questions students may have.

WRITING ASSIGNMENT #2 *The Indian in the Cupboard*

PROMPT

Choose the type of folktale you want to write. Will it be a trickster tale in which a clever character outwits a foolish one, a tale of a talking animal that has special qualities, or a tale that explains why something happened. Choose whatever type of story appeals to you.

PREWRITING

1. List three characters who will be in your story. What are their names? Describe each.

Name	Physical Description	Personality Traits

2. Where does you story take place?_____

3. Which character has a problem?_____
   What is the problem?_____

4. Does your story contain a surprise? What?_____

5. Is there anything else special in your story?_____

6. Is there a lesson to be learned from your story? What?_____

7. Does your story explain how something came to be? What?_____

8. What are your characters doing when the story opens?_____

9. List the main things that happen in your story (in order)._____

DRAFTING
Start to write your story beginning with the opening you choose (#8 in Pre-writing). Write the action for the events that you planned in #9 of the pre-writing step. Include the other details you planned in the pre-writing steps. Try to use words that describe and action verbs to keep your story interesting.

PROMPT
When you finish the rough draft of your folktale, ask a student who sits near you to read it. After reading your rough draft, he/she should tell you what he/she liked best about your work, which parts were difficult to understand, and ways in which your work could be improved. Reread your paper considering your critic's comments, and make the corrections you think are necessary. Ask your classmate what he/she thought of each of the characters/events you chose for your assignment.

PROOFREADING
Do a final proofreading of your paper double-checking your grammar, spelling, organization, and the clarity of your ideas.

LESSON EIGHT

<u>Objectives</u>
1. To preview the study questions and vocabulary for Chapters 8-9
2. To read Chapters 8-9

<u>Activity #1</u>
Review the study questions and complete the vocabulary work for Chapters 8-9 together as a class.

<u>Activity #2</u>
Give students the remaining class time to read Chapters 8-9 silently. If they do not finish this assignment in class, they should do so for homework.

LESSON NINE

<u>Objectives</u>
1. To review the main events and ideas of Chapters 8-9
2. To introduce the group project

<u>Activity #1</u>
Discuss the answers to the study questions from Chapters 8-9 as previously directed.

<u>Activity #2</u>
Distribute the Group Project Assignment Sheets and discuss the directions in detail. Make the group assignments either by letting students choose the group they want to be in or by assigning students to groups. Show students where and how to find information and give them the remainder of this class period to find information about their topics.

GROUP PROJECT ASSIGNMENT SHEET *The Indian in the Cupboard*

INDIANS
Little Bear is from the Iroquois tribe of Indians and is the son of a chief. There were and are many different tribes of Indians. Some of these tribes include the Algonquin, Apache, Blackfoot, Cherokee, Cheyenne, Chinook, Comanche, Crow, Hopi, Huron, Nanticoke, Nantucket, Mojave, and Seminole.

There were also many famous Indians throughout history including Pocahontas, Sitting Bull, Crazy Horse, Iron Horse, Chief Joseph, and Geronimo to name a few.

COWBOYS
Boone is a cowboy. There were and are many famous (and not-so-famous) cowboys. Cowboys actually tended herds of cattle, but there is a lot of folklore about them, too. Sometimes people confuse real cowboys with the other people who were legends of the Wild West. Some topics related to cowboys are: Rodeos, Ranch Life, Cattle Drives, Famous Cowboys.

PIONEERS
There is another group of people who aren't a part of *The Indian in the Cupboard* but were very much a part of life with cowboys and Indians. They were the settlers or pioneers who were often farmers. Some topics related to pioneers are: Oregon Trail, Wagon Trains, Pony Express, Ghost Towns, Buffalo, Daniel Boone, Davey Crockett, Kit Carson, James Marshall, Fur Trading.

YOUR ASSIGNMENT
Each person in your group must choose a different topic.

1. Read about the topic from at least two different sources.

2. Fill out a Non-fiction Sheet for each of the two things you read.

3. Draw a picture related to your topic.

4. Complete Writing Assignment #3.

Meet with your group at least three times to talk about what you all have read and to create a presentation to make to the class about your group's topic. Your presentation has to include something from each person's reading. You may dress up, do a show and tell type presentation, use the computer and/or make a poster to add interest to your presentation.

NON-FICTION ASSIGNMENT SHEET *The Indian in the Cupboard*

Name_____ Date_____

Topic _____

Source of Information _____
               (Internet address/Site name, name of book or magazine article, etc.)

Name of article or web address_____

Summary of information found:

Your notes or comments:

WRITING ASSIGNMENT # 3 *The Indian in the Cupboard*

PROMPT
You are doing a group project about Indians, cowboys, or settler/pioneers. Your assignment is to write about what you have learned from reading about your topic within your group.

PRE-WRITING
Make a list of things you have learned from your reading. Are there things on the list that "go together" or are related in some way? These things should be organized close together in your composition. On your list, identify things that should go together. Number the items on your list so you know what order you want to use them in your composition. Keep related items together and use a logical order.

DRAFTING
My group is assigned to find out about _____.
I have chosen to read about _____,
and I have learned many things about (it, them).

Paragraph 2
Topic Sentence _____
_____

Fact _____
Fact _____

Paragraph 3
Topic Sentence _____
_____

Fact _____
Fact _____

Paragraph 4
Topic Sentence _____
_____

Fact _____
Fact _____

Concluding Paragraph Topic Sentence _____
_____

Sentence 2 _____
_____

Sentence 3 _____
_____

PROMPT

When you finish the rough draft of your composition, ask a student who sits near you to read it. After reading your rough draft, he/she should tell you what he/she liked best about your work, which parts were difficult to understand, and ways in which your work could be improved. Reread your paper considering your critic's comments, and make the corrections you think are necessary. Ask your classmate what he/she thought of each of the characters/events you chose for your assignment.

PROOFREADING

Do a final proofreading of your paper double-checking your grammar, spelling, organization, and the clarity of your ideas.

LESSON TEN

Objectives
1. To preview the study questions and vocabulary for Chapters 10-12
2. To read Chapters 10-12

Activity #1
Give students time to preview the study questions and do the vocabulary work for Chapters 10-12. Discuss and post the answers to the vocabulary so all students will have the correct answers for study purposes.

Activity #2
Students should use the class period to read Chapters 10-12. Students may read silently or in pairs to each other. This assignment should be completed as homework if not finished in class.

Students who finish reading early may work on their folktales or on their group project.

LESSON ELEVEN

Objectives
1. To review the main events and ideas of Chapters 10-12
2. To discuss the evolving friendships among the main characters

Activity #1
Discuss the answers to the study questions from Chapters 10-12 as previously directed.

Activity #2
Return to the concept of friendship. Lead a class discussion using the following questions: Omri shared his secret with Patrick and let him keep Boone. What does this imply about their friendship? At this point in the book, how would you characterize their friendship? Do you think they will remain friends? Why or why not? Would you describe Omri and Little Bear as friends? Why or why not? How do responsibility and loyalty enter into each of the friendships? How has Omri changed in ways Patrick has not?

Activity #3
Assign each student a chapter to skim to locate passages from the book that demonstrate friendship and loyalty among the characters. After they have had time to skim through the story, ask for examples they found and make a list on the board for students to copy. Discuss the examples as appropriate. Encourage students to add to the list as they continue to read the book.

Activity #4
If time remains, students may meet in their project groups to discuss their reading.

LESSON TWELVE

<u>Objectives</u>
1. To preview the study questions and vocabulary for Chapters 13-14
2. To read Chapters 13-14

<u>Activity #1</u>
Review the study questions and complete the vocabulary work for Chapters 13-14 together as a class.

<u>Activity #2</u>
Students should use the class period to read Chapters 13-14. Students may read silently or in pairs to each other. Encourage them to add more examples of friendship and loyalty to their lists. This assignment should be completed as homework if not finished in class. Also, tell students that they will have time during the next class session to work on the group project.

LESSON THIRTEEN

<u>Objectives</u>
    1. To review the main events and ideas of Chapters 13-14
    2. To work on the group project

<u>Activity #1</u>
Discuss the answers to the study questions from Chapters 13-14 as previously directed. Allow time for students to share passages from the book that demonstrate friendship and loyalty among the characters.

<u>Activity #2</u>
Devote the remainder of the class period to the group project. Depending on their progress, you may need to add an additional session.

Ask how many students have:
1. read two articles about their topics
2. completed the Non-fiction Assignment Sheet for each article
3. written a paragraph summarizing their reading
4. drawn a picture related to their reading

If most students have completed all of these, allow groups to meet to plan their presentation in the remaining class time. If most have NOT completed 1-4, then allow most of the class time for independent work on this project and only about 10-15 minutes for a group meeting at the end of class.

LESSON FOURTEEN

Objectives
1. To preview the study questions and vocabulary for Chapters 15-16
2. To read Chapters 15-16

Activity #1
Give students time to preview the study questions and do the vocabulary work for Chapters 15-16. Discuss and post the answers to the vocabulary worksheet so all students will have the correct answers for study purposes.

Activity #2
Students should use the class period to read chapters 15-16. Students may read silently or in pairs to each other. Encourage them to add more examples of friendship and loyalty to their lists. This assignment should be completed as homework if not finished in class. Also, tell students that they will have time during the next class session to work on the group project.

Also, tell students that Writing Assignment #2 (their folktales) will be due after the unit test (Lesson Twenty). If students finish reading early they should work on their folktales or on the group project.

LESSON FIFTEEN

<u>Objectives</u>
1. To review the main event and ideas of Chapters 15-16
2. To work on the group project

<u>Activity #1</u>
Discuss the answers to the study questions from Chapters 15-16 as previously directed. Allow time for students to share passages from the book that demonstrate friendship and loyalty among the characters.

<u>Activity #2</u>
Devote the remainder of the class period to the group project. Most of the independent work should be done by now and most of this class time should be devoted to the groups working on their presentations.

Tell students they will have one more opportunity to meet as a group.

LESSON SIXTEEN

Objectives
1. To answer higher-level comprehension questions including interpretation, critical analysis, and personal response
2. To use a variety of thinking skills that add to the understanding of the novel
3. To discuss the answers to the questions

Activity

Choose the questions from the Extra Discussion Questions/Writing Assignments which seem most appropriate for your students. A class discussion of these questions is most effective if students have been given the opportunity to formulate answers to the questions prior to the discussion. Therefore, you may either have all the students formulate answers to all the questions, divide your class into groups and assign one or more questions to each group, or you could assign one question to each student in your class. The option you choose will make a difference in the amount of class time needed for this activity.

NOTE: The use of graphic organizers may be helpful to students in preparing their answers. Encourage them to use any diagrams or graphics that they feel are necessary.

EXTRA DISCUSSION QUESTIONS/WRITING ASSIGNMENTS *Indian in the Cupboard*

Interpretive
1. What are the main conflicts in the story? Do they get resolved by the end of the book?
2. Where is the high point (climax) of the story?
3. Describe Lynne Reid Banks' writing style. How does it affect the story?
4. How would you describe Omri's personality? Use situations from the book to explain your answer.
5. How did the setting of the story add to the plot?
6. Note some examples of foreshadowing.
7. Compare and contrast Little Bear and Boone.
8. Besides friendship, what are some other themes within the book?

Critical
9. Do you think the author's portrayal of Little Bear was accurate?
10. Why did Omri do almost everything Little Bear asked?
11. Do you think Omri's mother knew the key was magic? Use examples from the book to justify your response.
12. How did Omri and Patrick change as a result of their experiences with Little Bear and Boone?
13. How do you think Little Bear felt about Boone?
14. Describe some lessons Omri learned about life.
15. In what ways did Omri and Patrick remain loyal to each other?

Critical/Personal Response
16. Which character (Boone or Little Bear) would be easier to care for? Why?
17. Would you rather be Omri's or Patrick's friend? Why?
18. What do you think happened to Mr. Johnson, the headmaster?
19. How old is Little Bear? What about Boone? Why do you think they are that age?
20. How has Little Bear's disappearance affected his life back home? What about Boone's?
21. What might happen to Little Bear and Boone if they visited you for a day?

Personal Response
22. What was your reaction to the book? Did you like it? Would you recommend it?
23. Did you find the characters believable?
24. What do you think happens to the characters after the book ends?
25. Do you think Patrick and Omri will remain friends? Why or why not?
26. Do you think Patrick and Omri will put the cupboard and key to use again?
27. Whom would you choose to tell about Little Bear? Why?
28. If you could bring a toy to life, which toy would you select and why?
29. What did you learn from the friendships in the book that you could apply to your life?

QUOTATIONS *The Indian in the Cupboard*

1. "The unordinary one was the most interesting key in the whole collection, small with a complicated lock part and a fancy top."

2. "Tepee!" the Indian shouted. "I no live tepee. I live longhouse!"

3. "English good! Iroquois fight with English against French!"

4. He asked himself, swallowing repeatedly and feeling that just the same he might be sick, whether he wouldn't do better to put Little Bear back in the cupboard, lock the door, and turn him back into plastic, knife and all.

5. "Here! Where am I? Come back, you blokes--don't leave a chap alone in the dark!"

6. "Plass-tick?" Little Bear stared at the figure with its big feather headdress. "You make magic, get bow and arrows from plass-tick?"

7. "Dead," he said. "No breath. Heart stop. Old man. Gone to ancestors, very happy."

8. Omri debated with himself. He somehow felt that if he didn't share his secret with Patrick, their friendship would be over.

9. "Omri's friend, Little Bear's friend," said Little Bear magnanimously.

10. The burden of constant worry was beginning to wear him out.

11. He just knew, somehow, that something awful would happen if he let Patrick have his own way.

12. "You shore ain't no reg'lar hallucy-nation," he said. "I'm obliged to ya."

13. "Ah cain't start the day till Ah've had mah jug o' cawfee!"

14. Once again Omri felt their friendship trembling on the edge of destruction.

15. He thought back to the time, only a few days ago, when this had all started, and he had fondly imagined it was all going to be the greatest fun anybody ever had. Now he realized that it was more like a nightmare.

16. "Whur's the rows of desks? Whur's the slate 'n' bit o' chalk? Why ain't the teacher talkin'?"

17. "I'm going to put the key away somewhere so I won't be tempted; but it will always be there."

LESSON SEVENTEEN

<u>Objective</u>
　　To work on the group project

<u>Activity</u>
Remind students this is the last time they will meet to complete the group project requirements. They will present their findings during the next class.

LESSON EIGHTEEN

<u>Objective</u>
    To present group projects

<u>Activity</u>
Have each group share the results of its group project. While each group presents, evaluate the presentation using the group project evaluation. After all the groups have presented, hold a brief class discussion about the information students have just heard.

Group Presentation Evaluation Sheet

Each of the following will be graded on a scale of 1-5, with 1 being the lowest; each is worth 20% of the overall grade.

Part I: individual contribution during the preparation time in class (This has been monitored during in-class group work)

Part II: individual contribution to the biographical portion of the group project and its presentation (how well he/she is prepared to read from his/her research materials)

Part III: individual contributed to the presentation about his/her selected story

Part IV: individual portion of the writing assignment was completed (analysis)

Part V: individual has provided all of his/her necessary portions of the group project (this includes individual drawing)

Student Name	Part I	Part II	Part III	Part IV	Part V	Total Score

LESSON NINETEEN

<u>Objective</u>
   To pull together and review all of the vocabulary work done in this unit

<u>Activity</u>
Choose one (or more) of the vocabulary review activities listed below and spend your class period as directed in the activity. Some of the materials for these review activities are located in the Vocabulary Resource Materials section in this LitPlan.

VOCABULARY REVIEW ACTIVITIES

1. Divide your class into two teams and have an old-fashioned spelling or definition bee.

2. Give each of your students (or students in groups of two, three or four) an *Indian in the Cupboard* Vocabulary Word Search Puzzle. The person (group) to find all of the vocabulary words in the puzzle first wins.

3. Give students *The Indian in the Cupboard* Vocabulary Word Search Puzzle without the word list. The person or group to find the most vocabulary words in the puzzle wins.

4. Use *The Indian in the Cupboard* Vocabulary Crossword Puzzle. Put the puzzle onto a transparency on the overhead projector (so everyone can see it), and do the puzzle together as a class.

5. Give students *The Indian in the Cupboard* Vocabulary Matching Worksheet to do.

6. Divide your class into two teams. Use *The Indian in the Cupboard* vocabulary words with their letters jumbled as a word list. Student 1 from Team A faces off against Student 1 from Team B. You write the first jumbled word on the board. The first student (1A or 1B) to unscramble the word wins the chance for his/her team to score points. If 1A wins the jumble, go to student 2A and give him/her a definition. He/she must give you the correct spelling of the vocabulary word which fits that definition. If he/she does, Team A scores a point, and you give student 3A a definition for which you expect a correctly spelled matching vocabulary word. Continue giving Team A definitions until some team member makes an incorrect response. An incorrect response sends the game back to the jumbled-word face off, this time with students 2A and 2B. Instead of repeating giving definitions to the first few students of each team, continue with the student after the one who gave the last incorrect response on the team. For example, if Team B wins the jumbled-word face-off, and student 5B gave the last incorrect answer for Team B, you would start this round of definition questions with student 6B, and so on. The team with the most points wins!

7. Have students write a story in which they correctly use as many vocabulary words as possible. Have students read their compositions orally. Post the most original compositions on your bulletin board!

LESSON TWENTY

Objective
>To review the main events and ideas in *The Indian in the Cupboard*

Activity
Choose one of the following review games/activities and spend class time as directed there. Also, remind students that Writing Assignment #2 will be due at the end of the unit test in Lesson Twenty.

UNIT REVIEW ACTIVITIES

1. Ask the class to make up a unit test for *The Indian in the Cupboard*. The test should have 4 sections: matching, true/false, short answer, and essay. Students may use 1/2 of the class period to make the test and then swap papers and use the other 1/2 of the period to take a test a classmate has devised (open book). You may want to use the unit test included in this packet or take questions from the students' unit tests to formulate your own test.

2. Take 1/2 period for students to make up true and false questions (including the answers). Collect the papers and divide the class into two teams. Draw a big Tic-Tac-Toe board on the chalk board. Make one team X and one team O. Ask questions to each side, giving each student one turn. If the question is answered correctly, that student's team's letter (X or O) is placed in the box. If the answer is incorrect, no letter is placed in the box. The object is to get three in a row like Tic-Tac-Toe. You may want to keep track of the number of games won for each team.

3. Take 1/2 period for students to make up questions (true/false and short answer). Collect the questions. Divide the class into two teams. You'll alternate asking questions to individual members of teams A and B (like in a spelling bee). The question keeps going from A to B until it is correctly answered, then a new question is asked. A correct answer does not allow the team to get another question. Correct answers are +2 points; incorrect answers are -1 point.

4. Have students pair up and quiz each other from their study guides and class notes.

5. Give students a *The Indian in the Cupboard* crossword puzzle to complete.

6. Divide your class into two teams. Use *The Indian in the Cupboard* crossword words with their letters jumbled as a word list. Student 1 from Team A faces off against Student 1 from Team B. You write the first jumbled word on the board. The first student (1A or 1B) to unscramble the word wins the chance for his/her team to score points. If 1A wins the jumble, go to student 2A and give him/her a clue. He/she must give you the correct word which matches that clue. If he/she does, Team A scores a point, and you give student 3A a clue for which you expect another correct response. An incorrect response sends the game back to the jumbled-word face off, this time with students 2A and 2B. Instead of repeating giving clues to the first few students of each team, continue with the student after the one who gave the last incorrect response on the team. For example, if Team B wins the jumbled-word face-off, and student 5B gave the last incorrect answer for Team B, you would start this round of clue questions with student 6B and so on. The team with the most points wins!

7. Play *What's My Line?*. This is similar to the old television show. Students assume the roles of different characters from the novel. One student gives clues to the class, or to a panel of contestants. The contestants try to guess the identity of the guest. Students may enjoy assisting you in creating rules and procedures for the game.

8. Play *Jeopardy*. Divide the class into two groups. Assign each group a category or chapter from the novel and have them devise answers for that category. Play the game according to the television show procedures.

9. Play *Drawing on the Details*. This is similar to *Pictionary*. Divide the class into teams. A student from one team draws a scene from the novel. (You may want to specify the book or section.) Drawings should be kept simple, to keep the pace lively. Students in the opposing team locate the scene in their books and read it aloud. If they are incorrect, the illustrator's team has a chance to guess. Involve students in setting up a scoring system and any other necessary rules.

LESSON TWENTY-ONE

Objective
To test the students' understanding of the main ideas and themes in *The Indian in the Cupboard*

Activity #1
Distribute the unit tests, give students ample time to complete them, and collect the tests when students finish. Remember to collect assigned books prior to the end of the class period.

NOTES ABOUT THE UNIT TESTS IN THIS UNIT:

NOTE: There are 5 different unit tests included in the LitPlan Teacher Pack. Two are short answer, two are multiple choice. There is one advanced short answer test. The answers to the advanced short answer test will be based on the discussions you have had during class and should be graded accordingly. You should choose the tests and/or test parts which best suit your needs. Matching and short answer tests have answer keys. For essay type questions, grade according to your own criteria based on class discussions and the level of your students. Also, you will need to choose vocabulary words to read orally for the vocabulary section of the short answer tests.

Activity #2
Collect all test papers, assigned books, and Writing Assignment #2 prior to the end of the class period.

UNIT TESTS

The Indian in the Cupboard SHORT ANSWER UNIT TEST 1

I. MATCHING

____	1.	PATRICK	A.	Plastic cowboy who comes to life
____	2.	GILLON	B.	The headmaster: Mr. _____
____	3.	CHIEF	C.	If Omri got him this, Little Bear would dance.
____	4.	JOHNSON	D.	Omri's brother with the missing football shorts
____	5.	YAPP	E.	Little Bear and Omri; Little Bear and Boone are _____ Brothers
____	6.	TOMMY	F.	Little Bear belonged to this tribe.
____	7.	ADIEL	G.	Omri was afraid Little Bear would kill him.
____	8.	BEAR	H.	Source of the battle-ax
____	9.	APRIL	I.	Girl who teases Patrick at school
____	10.	BOONE	J.	Omri's brother who gave Omri the cupboard
____	11.	INDIAN	K.	He believed Omri was a character in a dream.
____	12.	IROQUOIS	L.	First World War soldier
____	13.	BELT	M.	Omri's friend
____	14.	SOLDIER	N.	Patrick's birthday gift to Omri: Plastic _____
____	15.	KNIGHT	O.	Little Bear gave Omri this as payment for his wife.
____	16.	COWBOY	P.	He died inside the cupboard: Indian _____.
____	17.	WIFE	Q.	Owner of the store where Omri purchased plastic figures
____	18.	STEALING	R.	Little Bear took thirty of these.
____	19.	BLOOD	S.	Indian in the cupboard: Little ____
____	20.	SCALPS	T.	Mr. Yapp accused Omri of this.

II. Short Answer

1. Why is Omri happy to receive the white metal cupboard from Gillon?

2. When Omri discovers the live Indian in the cupboard, why does he decide to keep it a secret?

3. How does the Indian introduce himself?

4. What type of house does Little Bear want to build?

5. Why does Omri tell Patrick about Little Bear?

6. What is Omri afraid will happen if Little Bear and the cowboy meet?

7. During art class, what does Omri learn about Boone?

8. What happens to Boone while he and Little Bear are watching a Western on TV?

9. Why does Little Bear give Omri his belt made of white beads?

10. What does Omri's mother tell him she will do with the key when he asks her to keep it for him?

III. Essay
1. How did Omri and Patrick change because of their experiences with Little Bear and Boone?

IV. Vocabulary
    A. Write the vocabulary words you are given. After writing them down, go back and write in their definitions.

Word	Definition
1	
2	
3	
4	
5	
6	
7	
8	
9	
10	

The Indian in the Cupboard SHORT ANSWER UNIT TEST 1 Answer Key

I. MATCHING

M	1.	PATRICK	A.	Plastic cowboy who comes to life
J	2.	GILLON	B.	The headmaster: Mr. _____
P	3.	CHIEF	C.	If Omri got him this, Little Bear would dance.
B	4.	JOHNSON	D.	Omri's brother with the missing football shorts
Q	5.	YAPP	E.	Little Bear and Omri; Little Bear and Boone are _____ Brothers
L	6.	TOMMY	F.	Little Bear belonged to this tribe.
D	7.	ADIEL	G.	Omri was afraid Little Bear would kill him.
S	8.	BEAR	H.	Source of the battle-ax
I	9.	APRIL	I.	Girl who teases Patrick at school
A	10.	BOONE	J.	Omri's brother who gave Omri the cupboard
N	11.	INDIAN	K.	He believed Omri was a character in a dream.
F	12.	IROQUOIS	L.	First World War soldier
O	13.	BELT	M.	Omri's friend
K	14.	SOLDIER	N.	Patrick's birthday gift to Omri: Plastic _____
H	15.	KNIGHT	O.	Little Bear gave Omri this as payment for his wife.
G	16.	COWBOY	P.	He died inside the cupboard: Indian _____.
C	17.	WIFE	Q.	Owner of the store where Omri purchased plastic figures
T	18.	STEALING	R.	Little Bear took thirty of these.
E	19.	BLOOD	S.	Indian in the cupboard: Little ____
R	20.	SCALPS	T.	Mr. Yapp accused Omri of this.

II. Short Answer
1. Why is Omri happy to receive the white metal cupboard from Gillon?
   Omri loves cupboards of any sort because it is fun to keep things in them.
2. When Omri discovers the live Indian in the cupboard, why does he decide to keep it a secret?
   Omri is afraid if he takes his eyes off the Indian he will vanish, and his family will laugh and accuse him of telling lies. He also feels if the Indian is really alive, this is the most marvelous thing that has ever happened to him, and he wants to keep it to himself, at least at first.
3. How does the Indian introduce himself?
   He points at himself proudly and says, "Little Bear. Iroquois brave. Son of chief."
4. What type of house does Little Bear want to build?
   He wants to build a longhouse.
5. Why does Omri tell Patrick about Little Bear?
   Omri doesn't want to lose Patrick's friendship. He also wants to show someone else his Indian.
6. What is Omri afraid will happen if Little Bear and the cowboy meet?
   Omri is afraid they will kill each other.
7. During art class, what does Omri learn about Boone?
   Art was Boone's best subject when he was in school, and he can draw very well.
8. What happens to Boone while he and Little Bear are watching a Western on TV?
   Angered by the killing of Indians in the Western TV show, Little Bear shoots Boone with an arrow.
9. Why does Little Bear give Omri his belt made of white beads?
   He gives Omri the belt as payment for his new wife.
10. What does Omri's mother tell him she will do with the key when he asks her to keep it for him?
    She tells him she will get a chain and wear it like she always meant to.

IV. Vocabulary
   Write the vocabulary words and definitions you will use for this test.

Word	Definition
1	
2	
3	
4	
5	
6	
7	
8	
9	
10	

The Indian in the Cupboard SHORT ANSWER UNIT TEST 2

I. Matching

____ 1. PATRICK A. Plastic cowboy who comes to life

____ 2. GILLON B. The headmaster: Mr. _____

____ 3. NATIONS C. Girl who teases Patrick at school

____ 4. CHIEF D. Boone's best subject in school

____ 5. JOHNSON E. He died inside the cupboard: Indian ____.

____ 6. BOOHOO F. Little Bear's wife: Bright ____

____ 7. YAPP G. Owner of the store where Omri purchased plastic figures

____ 8. TOMMY H. If Omri got him this, Little Bear would dance.

____ 9. ADIEL I. Omri's brother with the missing football shorts

____ 10. STARS J. Source of the battle-ax

____ 11. BEAR K. He believed Omri was a character in a dream.

____ 12. APRIL L. First World War soldier

____ 13. BOONE M. Omri's brother who gave Omri the cupboard

____ 14. INDIAN N. Patrick's birthday gift to Omri: Plastic _____

____ 15. IROQUOIS O. Boone's nickname

____ 16. SOLDIER P. Little Bear belonged to this tribe.

____ 17. KNIGHT Q. Indian in the cupboard: Little ____

____ 18. COWBOY R. Iroquois Indians were sometimes called this: The Five ____.

____ 19. WIFE S. Omri was afraid Little Bear would kill him.

____ 20. ART T. Omri's friend

II. Short Answer

1. What is special about the key Omri finds to lock the cupboard?

2. What is Omri's reaction when the Indian threatens to kill Omri if he touches the Indian?

3. What elements together magically bring toys to life?

4. Why does Omri consider turning Little Bear back into plastic?

5. When Little Bear realizes all the dangers outside, what does he request from Omri?

6. What does Omri have to do to get Little Bear to dance?

7. What happens after Mr. Johnson throws Omri out of his office?

8. Why does Adiel take the cupboard from Omri's room?

9. Why does Little Bear give Omri his belt made of white beads?

10. After Omri puts Little Bear, his wife, and Boone in the cupboard, why does Little Bear ask for Omri's hand?

III. Essay
1. What are the main conflicts in the story? Do they get resolved by the end of the book?

IV. Quotations: Explain the importance and meaning of the following quotations:

1. "English good! Iroquois fight with English against French!"

2. Omri debated with himself. He somehow felt that if he didn't share his secret with Patrick, their friendship would be over.

3. The burden of constant worry was beginning to wear him out.

4. Once again Omri felt their friendship trembling on the edge of destruction.

5. "I'm going to put the key away somewhere so I won't be tempted; but it will always be there."

V. Vocabulary
   A. Write the vocabulary words you are given. After writing them down, go back and write in their definitions.

Word	Definition
1	
2	
3	
4	
5	
6	
7	
8	
9	
10	

The Indian in the Cupboard SHORT ANSWER UNIT TEST 2 Answer Key

I. Matching

T	1.	PATRICK	A.	Plastic cowboy who comes to life
M	2.	GILLON	B.	The headmaster: Mr. _____
R	3.	NATIONS	C.	Girl who teases Patrick at school
E	4.	CHIEF	D.	Boone's best subject in school
B	5.	JOHNSON	E.	He died inside the cupboard: Indian _____.
O	6.	BOOHOO	F.	Little Bear's wife: Bright _____
G	7.	YAPP	G.	Owner of the store where Omri purchased plastic figures
L	8.	TOMMY	H.	If Omri got him this, Little Bear would dance.
I	9.	ADIEL	I.	Omri's brother with the missing football shorts
F	10.	STARS	J.	Source of the battle-ax
Q	11.	BEAR	K.	He believed Omri was a character in a dream.
C	12.	APRIL	L.	First World War soldier
A	13.	BOONE	M.	Omri's brother who gave Omri the cupboard
N	14.	INDIAN	N.	Patrick's birthday gift to Omri: Plastic _____
P	15.	IROQUOIS	O.	Boone's nickname
K	16.	SOLDIER	P.	Little Bear belonged to this tribe.
J	17.	KNIGHT	Q.	Indian in the cupboard: Little _____
S	18.	COWBOY	R.	Iroquois Indians were sometimes called this: The Five _____.
H	19.	WIFE	S.	Omri was afraid Little Bear would kill him.
D	20.	ART	T.	Omri's friend

II. Short Answer
1. What is special about the key Omri finds to lock the cupboard?
   The key was to his great-grandmother's jewel box. Omri's mother had worn it around her neck until the ribbon broke, and she almost lost it.
2. What is Omri's reaction when the Indian threatens to kill Omri if he touches the Indian?
   Even though there is a vast difference in their sizes and strengths, Omri respects the Indian and is afraid.
3. What elements together magically bring toys to life?
   The toys must be plastic and the cupboard must be locked with Omri's great-grandmother's key.
4. Why does Omri consider turning Little Bear back into plastic?
   After a discussion of war and scalping, Omri realizes that Little Bear is real, not a toy or an actor.
5. When Little Bear realizes all the dangers outside, what does he request from Omri?
   Little Bear asks Omri for Indian weapons: bow, arrows, and a club. He also asks for a gun.
6. What does Omri have to do to get Little Bear to dance?
   Omri must get Little Bear a wife and then he will dance.
7. What happens after Mr. Johnson throws Omri out of his office?
   Patrick shows Little Bear to Mr. Johnson.
8. Why does Adiel take the cupboard from Omri's room?
   Adiel got detention for not having his football shorts. He thinks Omri has taken them, so he takes the cupboard to teach Omri a lesson.
9. Why does Little Bear give Omri his belt made of white beads?
   He gives Omri the belt as payment for his new wife.
10. After Omri puts Little Bear, his wife, and Boone in the cupboard, why does Little Bear ask for Omri's hand?
    Before going back to his own time Little Bear wants to make Omri his blood brother.

V. Vocabulary
   Write the vocabulary words and definitions you will use for this test.

Word	Definition
1	
2	
3	
4	
5	
6	
7	
8	
9	
10	

The Indian in the Cupboard ADVANCED SHORT ANSWER UNIT TEST

I. Matching

____ 1. PATRICK   A. Omri was afraid Little Bear would kill him.

____ 2. GILLON   B. He believed Omri was a character in a dream.

____ 3. CHIEF   C. Plastic cowboy who comes to life

____ 4. JOHNSON   D. Source of the battle-ax

____ 5. HALLUCY   E. First World War soldier

____ 6. BOOHOO   F. Little Bear's wife: Bright ____

____ 7. YAPP   G. Omri's brother who gave Omri the cupboard

____ 8. SISTERS   H. Iroquois house

____ 9. LONGHOUSE   I. Omri's brother with the missing football shorts

____ 10. TOMMY   J. Little Bear belonged to this tribe.

____ 11. ADIEL   K. Indian in the cupboard: Little ____

____ 12. STARS   L. Girl who teases Patrick at school

____ 13. BEAR   M. If Omri got him this, Little Bear would dance.

____ 14. APRIL   N. Maize, beans, and squash: 3 _____

____ 15. BOONE   O. Owner of the store where Omri purchased plastic figures

____ 16. IROQUOIS   P. The headmaster: Mr. _____

____ 17. SOLDIER   Q. He died inside the cupboard: Indian _____.

____ 18. KNIGHT   R. Boone's nickname

____ 19. COWBOY   S. Boone's nickname for Omri: _____-Nation

____ 20. WIFE   T. Omri's friend

II. Short Answer
1. What are the main conflicts in the story? Do they get resolved by the end of the book?

2. Where is the high point (climax) of the story?

3. "Foreshadowing" means you get a hint of something to come in the story. What is one example of this from *The Indian in the Cupboard?*

4. Tell how Little Bear and Boone are alike and how they are different.

5. How did Omri and Patrick change because of their experiences with Little Bear and Boone?

III. Quotations: Explain the importance and meaning of the following quotations:

1. "English good! Iroquois fight with English against French!"

2. He asked himself, swallowing repeatedly and feeling that just the same he might be sick, whether he wouldn't do better to put Little Bear back in the cupboard, lock the door, and turn him back into plastic, knife and all.

3. "You shore ain't no reg'lar hallucy-nation," he said. "I'm obliged to ya."

4. He thought back to the time, only a few days ago, when this had all started, and he had fondly imagined it was all going to be the greatest fun anybody ever had. Now he realized that it was more like a nightmare.

5. "I'm going to put the key away somewhere so I won't be tempted; but it will always be there."

IV. Essay
1. What are the main conflicts in the story? Do they get resolved by the end of the book?

V. Vocabulary
   A. Write the vocabulary words you are given. After writing them down, go back and write in their definitions.

Word	Definition
1	
2	
3	
4	
5	
6	
7	
8	
9	
10	

   B. Write a paragraph about the book using 8 of the 10 vocabulary words above.

The Indian in the Cupboard ADVANCED SHORT ANSWER UNIT TEST Answer Key

I. Matching

T	1.	PATRICK	A.	Omri was afraid Little Bear would kill him.
G	2.	GILLON	B.	He believed Omri was a character in a dream.
Q	3.	CHIEF	C.	Plastic cowboy who comes to life
P	4.	JOHNSON	D.	Source of the battle-ax
S	5.	HALLUCY	E.	First World War soldier
R	6.	BOOHOO	F.	Little Bear's wife: Bright _____
O	7.	YAPP	G.	Omri's brother who gave Omri the cupboard
N	8.	SISTERS	H.	Iroquois house
H	9.	LONGHOUSE	I.	Omri's brother with the missing football shorts
E	10.	TOMMY	J.	Little Bear belonged to this tribe.
I	11.	ADIEL	K.	Indian in the cupboard: Little _____
F	12.	STARS	L.	Girl who teases Patrick at school
K	13.	BEAR	M.	If Omri got him this, Little Bear would dance.
L	14.	APRIL	N.	Maize, beans, and squash: 3 _____
C	15.	BOONE	O.	Owner of the store where Omri purchased plastic figures
J	16.	IROQUOIS	P.	The headmaster: Mr. _____
B	17.	SOLDIER	Q.	He died inside the cupboard: Indian _____.
D	18.	KNIGHT	R.	Boone's nickname
A	19.	COWBOY	S.	Boone's nickname for Omri: _____-Nation
M	20.	WIFE	T.	Omri's friend

V. Vocabulary

Write the vocabulary words and definitions you will use for this test.

Word	Definition
1	
2	
3	
4	
5	
6	
7	
8	
9	
10	

The Indian in the Cupboard MULTIPLE CHOICE UNIT TEST 1

I. Matching

____ 1.	PATRICK	A.	Girl who teases Patrick at school
____ 2.	GILLON	B.	Omri was afraid Little Bear would kill him.
____ 3.	CHIEF	C.	Owner of the store where Omri purchased plastic figures
____ 4.	JOHNSON	D.	Little Bear belonged to this tribe.
____ 5.	HALLUCY	E.	Omri's brother with the missing football shorts
____ 6.	BOOHOO	F.	Boone's nickname for Omri: _____-Nation
____ 7.	YAPP	G.	Little Bear's wife: Bright ____
____ 8.	SISTERS	H.	Plastic cowboy who comes to life
____ 9.	LONGHOUSE	I.	The headmaster: Mr. _____
____ 10.	TOMMY	J.	Iroquois house
____ 11.	ADIEL	K.	Maize, beans, and squash: 3 _____
____ 12.	STARS	L.	He believed Omri was a character in a dream.
____ 13.	BEAR	M.	Omri's friend
____ 14.	APRIL	N.	First World War soldier
____ 15.	BOONE	O.	If Omri got him this, Little Bear would dance.
____ 16.	IROQUOIS	P.	Source of the battle-ax
____ 17.	SOLDIER	Q.	Indian in the cupboard: Little ____
____ 18.	KNIGHT	R.	Omri's brother who gave Omri the cupboard
____ 19.	COWBOY	S.	He died inside the cupboard: Indian _____.
____ 20.	WIFE	T.	Boone's nickname

II. Multiple Choice

1. What does Omri's mother tell him she will do with the key when he asks her to keep it for him?
    A. She tells him that it is meant to be with the cupboard.
    B. She tells him she will get a chain and wear it like she always meant to.
    C. She tells him she will put it in a safe so that he cannot get to it unless he is really sure he wants it.
    D. She tells him that it will be in her jewelry box if he ever needs it.

2. When Omri discovers the live Indian in the cupboard why does he decide to keep it a secret?
    A. The Indian told him to keep it a secret.
    B. Omri is afraid his family will laugh and accuse him of telling lies.
    C. He doesn't want his mother to take the key away.
    D. He know he is just dreaming.

3. How does the Indian introduce himself?
    A. He points at himself proudly and says, "Little Bear. Iroquois chief."
    B. He points at himself proudly and says, "Little Bear. Iroquois brave. Son of chief."
    C. He points at himself proudly and says, "Big Bear. Iroquois brave. Son of chief."
    D. He points at himself proudly and says, "Big Bear. Iroquois chief."

4. What type of house does Little Bear want to build?
    A. He wants to build a longhouse.
    B. He wants to build a wigwam.
    C. He wants to build a tepee.
    D. He wants to build a lodge.

5. Why does Omri tell Patrick about Little Bear?
    A. Omri needs someone to help him manage all the responsibilities.
    B. Since Patrick enjoys history, Omri wants to get some advice from him about Iroquois Indians.
    C. Omri feels that he can trust Patrick with his secret.
    D. Omri doesn't want to lose Patrick's friendship. He also wants to show someone else his Indian.

6. What is Omri afraid will happen if Little Bear and the cowboy meet?
   A. Omri is afraid they will be scared of one another.
   B. Omri is afraid they will kill each other.
   C. Omri is afraid they will band together and try to escape.
   D. Omri is afraid they will become friends and Little Bear won't want to talk to him (Omri) anymore.

7. During art class, what does Omri learn about Boone?
   A. Boone took art classes in school and hated them.
   B. Art was Boone's best subject when he was in school, and he can draw very well.
   C. Boone cannot tell the difference between the paints, so he must be colorblind.
   D. Boone is allergic to the chemicals in modern paper. He begins to break out in a rash.

8. What happens to Boone while he and Little Bear are watching a Western on TV?
   A. Angered by the killing of Indians in the Western TV show, Little Bear shoots Boone with an arrow.
   B. Boone sees the cowboys on TV and it reminds him of his old life. He begins to feel very homesick.
   C. Patrick gets up to get a drink and when he comes back he accidentally sits on Boone.
   D. Boone falls asleep and slips between the couch cushions. Omri and Patrick can't find him.

9. Why does Little Bear give Omri his belt made of white beads?
   A. He gives Omri the belt to give to Boone.
   B. He gives Omri the belt as a peace offering.
   C. He gives Omri the belt to bring to art class.
   D. He gives Omri the belt as payment for his new wife.

10. Why is Omri happy to receive the white metal cupboard from Gillon?
    A. Gillon has never given Omri a gift, so he is happy to get anything from Gillon.
    B. Omri loves cupboards of any sort because it is fun to keep things in them.
    C. Omri will keep all his medication in it.
    D. Omri knows it is all Gillon can afford.

III. Essay
1. How did Omri and Patrick change because of their experiences with Little Bear and Boone?

IV. Vocabulary

___ 1. COHERENT   A. Unbelieving
___ 2. INTRICATE   B. Plural of penny
___ 3. APPALLED   C. Sources of potential harm
___ 4. COAXED   D. Sarcastic
___ 5. RELUCTANT   E. Numerous
___ 6. FOREBODING   F. Eating any kind of food, including both plants and animals
___ 7. MAIZE   G. Stared in open-mouthed surprise
___ 8. PENCE   H. Logical
___ 9. INCREDULOUS I. Perplexed
___ 10. GAPED   J. Hesitant
___ 11. RAVENOUSLY K. A feeling of hopelessness
___ 12. TETHERED   L. Tied with a rope or chain
___ 13. TRUCE   M. Corn
___ 14. SNIDE   N. Shocked
___ 15. PERSECUTOR O. Oppressor; tyrant
___ 16. FLUMMOXED   P. Hungrily
___ 17. MYRIAD   Q. An agreed break in any type of dispute or feud
___ 18. DESPAIR   R. Persuaded gently
___ 19. PERILS   S. Containing many details or small parts that are skillfully made
___ 20. OMNIVOROUS T. A feeling that something bad is going to happen

The Indian in the Cupboard MULTIPLE CHOICE UNIT TEST 1 Answer Key

I. Matching

M	1.	PATRICK	A.	Girl who teases Patrick at school
R	2.	GILLON	B.	Omri was afraid Little Bear would kill him.
S	3.	CHIEF	C.	Owner of the store where Omri purchased plastic figures
I	4.	JOHNSON	D.	Little Bear belonged to this tribe.
F	5.	HALLUCY	E.	Omri's brother with the missing football shorts
T	6.	BOOHOO	F.	Boone's nickname for Omri: _____-Nation
C	7.	YAPP	G.	Little Bear's wife: Bright ____
K	8.	SISTERS	H.	Plastic cowboy who comes to life
J	9.	LONGHOUSE	I.	The headmaster: Mr. _____
N	10.	TOMMY	J.	Iroquois house
E	11.	ADIEL	K.	Maize, beans, and squash: 3 _____
G	12.	STARS	L.	He believed Omri was a character in a dream.
Q	13.	BEAR	M.	Omri's friend
A	14.	APRIL	N.	First World War soldier
H	15.	BOONE	O.	If Omri got him this, Little Bear would dance.
D	16.	IROQUOIS	P.	Source of the battle-ax
L	17.	SOLDIER	Q.	Indian in the cupboard: Little ____
P	18.	KNIGHT	R.	Omri's brother who gave Omri the cupboard
B	19.	COWBOY	S.	He died inside the cupboard: Indian _____.
O	20.	WIFE	T.	Boone's nickname

II. Multiple Choice

B 1. What does Omri's mother tell him she will do with the key when he asks her to keep it for him?
   A. She tells him that it is meant to be with the cupboard.
   B. She tells him she will get a chain and wear it like she always meant to.
   C. She tells him she will put it in a safe so that he cannot get to it unless he is really sure he wants it.
   D. She tells him that it will be in her jewelry box if he ever needs it.

B 2. When Omri discovers the live Indian in the cupboard why does he decide to keep it a secret?
   A. The Indian told him to keep it a secret.
   B. Omri is afraid his family will laugh and accuse him of telling lies.
   C. He doesn't want his mother to take the key away.
   D. He know he is just dreaming.

B 3. How does the Indian introduce himself?
   A. He points at himself proudly and says, "Little Bear. Iroquois chief."
   B. He points at himself proudly and says, "Little Bear. Iroquois brave. Son of chief."
   C. He points at himself proudly and says, "Big Bear. Iroquois brave. Son of chief."
   D. He points at himself proudly and says, "Big Bear. Iroquois chief."

A 4. What type of house does Little Bear want to build?
   A. He wants to build a longhouse.
   B. He wants to build a wigwam.
   C. He wants to build a tepee.
   D. He wants to build a lodge.

D 5. Why does Omri tell Patrick about Little Bear?
   A. Omri needs someone to help him manage all the responsibilities.
   B. Since Patrick enjoys history, Omri wants to get some advice from him about Iroquois Indians.
   C. Omri feels that he can trust Patrick with his secret.
   D. Omri doesn't want to lose Patrick's friendship. He also wants to show someone else his Indian.

B 6. What is Omri afraid will happen if Little Bear and the cowboy meet?
- A. Omri is afraid they will be scared of one another.
- B. Omri is afraid they will kill each other.
- C. Omri is afraid they will band together and try to escape.
- D. Omri is afraid they will become friends and Little Bear won't want to talk to him (Omri) anymore.

B 7. During art class, what does Omri learn about Boone?
- A. Boone took art classes in school and hated them.
- B. Art was Boone's best subject when he was in school, and he can draw very well.
- C. Boone cannot tell the difference between the paints, so he must be colorblind.
- D. Boone is allergic to the chemicals in modern paper. He begins to break out in a rash.

A 8. What happens to Boone while he and Little Bear are watching a Western on TV?
- A. Angered by the killing of Indians in the Western TV show, Little Bear shoots Boone with an arrow.
- B. Boone sees the cowboys on TV and it reminds him of his old life. He begins to feel very homesick.
- C. Patrick gets up to get a drink and when he comes back he accidentally sits on Boone.
- D. Boone falls asleep and slips between the couch cushions. Omri and Patrick can't find him.

D 9. Why does Little Bear give Omri his belt made of white beads?
- A. He gives Omri the belt to give to Boone.
- B. He gives Omri the belt as a peace offering.
- C. He gives Omri the belt to bring to art class.
- D. He gives Omri the belt as payment for his new wife.

B 10. Why is Omri happy to receive the white metal cupboard from Gillon?
- A. Gillon has never given Omri a gift, so he is happy to get anything from Gillon.
- B. Omri loves cupboards of any sort because it is fun to keep things in them.
- C. Omri will keep all his medication in it.
- D. Omri knows it is all Gillon can afford.

IV. Vocabulary

H	1.	COHERENT	A.	Unbelieving
S	2.	INTRICATE	B.	Plural of penny
N	3.	APPALLED	C.	Sources of potential harm
R	4.	COAXED	D.	Sarcastic
J	5.	RELUCTANT	E.	Numerous
T	6.	FOREBODING	F.	Eating any kind of food, including both plants and animals
M	7.	MAIZE	G.	Stared in open-mouthed surprise
B	8.	PENCE	H.	Logical
A	9.	INCREDULOUS	I.	Perplexed
G	10.	GAPED	J.	Hesitant
P	11.	RAVENOUSLY	K.	A feeling of hopelessness
L	12.	TETHERED	L.	Tied with a rope or chain
Q	13.	TRUCE	M.	Corn
D	14.	SNIDE	N.	Shocked
O	15.	PERSECUTOR	O.	Oppressor; tyrant
I	16.	FLUMMOXED	P.	Hungrily
E	17.	MYRIAD	Q.	An agreed break in any type of dispute or feud
K	18.	DESPAIR	R.	Persuaded gently
C	19.	PERILS	S.	Containing many details or small parts that are skillfully made
F	20.	OMNIVOROUS	T.	A feeling that something bad is going to happen

The Indian in the Cupboard MULTIPLE CHOICE UNIT TEST 2

I. Matching

____ 1. PATRICK   A.   Owner of the store where Omri purchased plastic figures

____ 2. GILLON   B.   Patrick's birthday gift to Omri: Plastic _____

____ 3. NATIONS   C.   Girl who teases Patrick at school

____ 4. CHIEF   D.   Plastic cowboy who comes to life

____ 5. JOHNSON   E.   Iroquois Indians were sometimes called this: The Five _____.

____ 6. HALLUCY   F.   Omri was afraid Little Bear would kill him.

____ 7. BOOHOO   G.   First World War soldier

____ 8. YAPP   H.   Boone's nickname

____ 9. SISTERS   I.   He believed Omri was a character in a dream.

____ 10. TOMMY   J.   Omri's friend

____ 11. ADIEL   K.   If Omri got him this, Little Bear would dance.

____ 12. STARS   L.   Omri's brother who gave Omri the cupboard

____ 13. BEAR   M.   Source of the battle-ax

____ 14. APRIL   N.   Maize, beans, and squash: 3 _____

____ 15. BOONE   O.   Indian in the cupboard: Little ____

____ 16. INDIAN   P.   Little Bear's wife: Bright ____

____ 17. SOLDIER   Q.   Omri's brother with the missing football shorts

____ 18. KNIGHT   R.   He died inside the cupboard: Indian _____.

____ 19. COWBOY   S.   The headmaster: Mr. _____

____ 20. WIFE   T.   Boone's nickname for Omri: _____-Nation

134

II. Multiple Choice

1. After Omri puts Little Bear, his wife, and Boone in the cupboard, why does Little Bear ask for Omri's hand?
    A. Little Bear puts a feather in Omri's hand so that he will never forget Little Bear.
    B. Before going back to his own time Little Bear wants to make Omri his blood brother.
    C. Little Bear wants to thank Omri for protecting him, but he doesn't know the words to say. He shakes Omri's hand and Omri understands.
    D. Before going back to his own time Little Bear wants to thank Omri again for getting him a wife.

2. What is Omri's reaction when the Indian threatens to kill Omri if he touches the Indian?
    A. Omri throws the Indian back into the cupboard and locks the door.
    B. Omri pins the Indian down with his finger.
    C. Even though there is a vast difference in their sizes and strengths, Omri respects the Indian and is afraid.
    D. Omri yells at the Indian that he is not afraid and the Indian hides in the cupboard.

3. What elements together magically bring toys to life?
    A. The cupboard had to be opened with Omri's great-grandmother's key and the toys had to be made of metal.
    B. The toys had to be made of plastic and appear realistic to come alive.
    C. The toys must be made of plastic and the cupboard must be locked with Omri's great-grandmother's key.
    D. The toys had to be made of plastic and placed upside down in the cupboard.

4. Why does Omri consider turning Little Bear back into plastic?
    A. He knows he will not be able to keep Little Bear a secret.
    B. Little Bear threatens to kill Omri.
    C. After a discussion of war and scalping, Omri realizes that Little Bear is too dangerous.
    D. After a discussion of war and scalping, Omri realizes that Little Bear is real, not a toy or an actor.

5. When Little Bear realizes all the dangers outside, what does he request from Omri?
    A. He asks for steel knives, spears, and cannons.
    B. He asks Omri for Indian weapons: bow, arrows, and a club. He also asks for a gun.
    C. He asks for fire, food, and water.
    D. He pleads for Omri to locate more Iroquois Indians to help him set up the new village.

6. What does Omri have to do to get Little Bear to dance?
    A. Omri must get Little Bear a new gun.
    B. Omri must feed him.
    C. Omri must turn Boone back into plastic.
    D. Omri must get Little Bear a wife.

7. What happens after Mr. Johnson throws Omri out of his office?
    A. Omri runs straight home.
    B. Patrick shows Little Bear to Mr. Johnson.
    C. Mr. Johnson gives Patrick detention for causing trouble.
    D. Patrick tells Mr. Johnson that Omri is crazy and thinks his toys can come to life.

8. Why does Adiel take the cupboard from Omri's room?
    A. Adiel has always liked the cupboard and thinks he deserves it just as much as Omri does.
    B. Adiel hears a rumor at school that Omri has a magical cupboard. He wants to see if the rumor is true.
    C. Adiel needs something to put his football trophies in. Since the cupboard is empty, he assumes Omri is not using it.
    D. Adiel got detention for not having his football shorts. He thinks Omri has taken them, so he takes the cupboard to teach Omri a lesson.

9. Why does Little Bear give Omri his belt made of white beads?
    A. He gives Omri the belt to bring to art class.
    B. He gives Omri the belt as payment for his new wife.
    C. He gives Omri the belt to give to Boone.
    D. He gives Omri the belt as a peace offering.

10. What is special about the key Omri finds to lock the cupboard?
    A. The key was to his grandmother's jewel box. Omri's mother wears it on a ribbon around her neck to keep it safe.
    B. The key was to his great-grandmother's jewel box. Omri's mother had worn it around her neck until the ribbon broke, and she almost lost it.
    C. The key was to his grandfather's safe. Omri's mother wears it on a chain around her neck to keep it from getting lost.
    D. The key was to his great-grandfather's desk. Omri's mother had worn it around her neck until the ribbon broke, and she almost lost it.

III. Vocabulary

____ 1. COHERENT   A. Enraged
____ 2. SCORN   B. To fall ill again after seeming to have made a recovery
____ 3. LITHELY   C. Replied in quick response to something someone has said
____ 4. FOREBODING   D. Immobile with fear
____ 5. TOURNIQUET   E. Bending easily
____ 6. PENCE   F. A thin rod or bar on which meat is pierced for broiling or roasting over a fire
____ 7. HECTORING   G. A euphoric state in which somebody is overwhelmed by happiness and unaware of anything else
____ 8. SPIT   H. A feeling that something bad is going to happen
____ 9. PETRIFIED   I. Open to physical danger or harm
____ 10. INFURIATED   J. Indebted to do something for someone
____ 11. OBLIGED   K. An agreed break in any type of dispute or feud
____ 12. RETORTED   L. Extremely small
____ 13. TRUCE   M. A tight band applied around an arm or a leg to stop bleeding
____ 14. APPREHENSION   N. Speaking in a domineering tone
____ 15. MINUTE   O. Logical
____ 16. RAPTURE   P. A feeling of anxiety or fear that something bad is going to occur
____ 17. DISMAY   Q. Puzzled
____ 18. VULNERABLE   R. To dishearten, alarm, cause loss of courage
____ 19. RELAPSE   S. A feeling of dislike
____ 20. BEMUSED   T. Plural of penny

IV. Essay
1. How would you describe Omri's personality? Use situations from the book to explain your answer.

The Indian in the Cupboard MULTIPLE CHOICE UNIT TEST 2 Answer Key

I. Matching

J	1.	PATRICK	A.	Owner of the store where Omri purchased plastic figures
L	2.	GILLON	B.	Patrick's birthday gift to Omri: Plastic _____
E	3.	NATIONS	C.	Girl who teases Patrick at school
R	4.	CHIEF	D.	Plastic cowboy who comes to life
S	5.	JOHNSON	E.	Iroquois Indians were sometimes called this: The Five _____.
T	6.	HALLUCY	F.	Omri was afraid Little Bear would kill him.
H	7.	BOOHOO	G.	First World War soldier
A	8.	YAPP	H.	Boone's nickname
N	9.	SISTERS	I.	He believed Omri was a character in a dream.
G	10.	TOMMY	J.	Omri's friend
Q	11.	ADIEL	K.	If Omri got him this, Little Bear would dance.
P	12.	STARS	L.	Omri's brother who gave Omri the cupboard
O	13.	BEAR	M.	Source of the battle-ax
C	14.	APRIL	N.	Maize, beans, and squash: 3 _____
D	15.	BOONE	O.	Indian in the cupboard: Little ____
B	16.	INDIAN	P.	Little Bear's wife: Bright ____
I	17.	SOLDIER	Q.	Omri's brother with the missing football shorts
M	18.	KNIGHT	R.	He died inside the cupboard: Indian _____.
F	19.	COWBOY	S.	The headmaster: Mr. _____
K	20.	WIFE	T.	Boone's nickname for Omri:_____-Nation

II. Multiple Choice

B 1. After Omri puts Little Bear, his wife, and Boone in the cupboard, why does Little Bear ask for Omri's hand?
   A. Little Bear puts a feather in Omri's hand so that he will never forget Little Bear.
   B. Before going back to his own time Little Bear wants to make Omri his blood brother.
   C. Little Bear wants to thank Omri for protecting him, but he doesn't know the words to say. He shakes Omri's hand and Omri understands.
   D. Before going back to his own time Little Bear wants to thank Omri again for getting him a wife.

C 2. What is Omri's reaction when the Indian threatens to kill Omri if he touches the Indian?
   A. Omri throws the Indian back into the cupboard and locks the door.
   B. Omri pins the Indian down with his finger.
   C. Even though there is a vast difference in their sizes and strengths, Omri respects the Indian and is afraid.
   D. Omri yells at the Indian that he is not afraid and the Indian hides in the cupboard.

C 3. What elements together magically bring toys to life?
   A. The cupboard had to be opened with Omri's great-grandmother's key and the toys had to be made of metal.
   B. The toys had to be made of plastic and appear realistic to come alive.
   C. The toys must be made of plastic and the cupboard must be locked with Omri's great-grandmother's key.
   D. The toys had to be made of plastic and placed upside down in the cupboard.

D 4. Why does Omri consider turning Little Bear back into plastic?
   A. He knows he will not be able to keep Little Bear a secret.
   B. Little Bear threatens to kill Omri.
   C. After a discussion of war and scalping, Omri realizes that Little Bear is too dangerous.
   D. After a discussion of war and scalping, Omri realizes that Little Bear is real, not a toy or an actor.

B 5. When Little Bear realizes all the dangers outside, what does he request from Omri?
- A. He asks for steel knives, spears, and cannons.
- B. He asks Omri for Indian weapons: bow, arrows, and a club. He also asks for a gun.
- C. He asks for fire, food, and water.
- D. He pleads for Omri to locate more Iroquois Indians to help him set up the new village.

D 6. What does Omri have to do to get Little Bear to dance?
- A. Omri must get Little Bear a new gun.
- B. Omri must feed him.
- C. Omri must turn Boone back into plastic.
- D. Omri must get Little Bear a wife.

B 7. What happens after Mr. Johnson throws Omri out of his office?
- A. Omri runs straight home.
- B. Patrick shows Little Bear to Mr. Johnson.
- C. Mr. Johnson gives Patrick detention for causing trouble.
- D. Patrick tells Mr. Johnson that Omri is crazy and thinks his toys can come to life.

D 8. Why does Adiel take the cupboard from Omri's room?
- A. Adiel has always liked the cupboard and thinks he deserves it just as much as Omri does.
- B. Adiel hears a rumor at school that Omri has a magical cupboard. He wants to see if the rumor is true.
- C. Adiel needs something to put his football trophies in. Since the cupboard is empty, he assumes Omri is not using it.
- D. Adiel got detention for not having his football shorts. He thinks Omri has taken them, so he takes the cupboard to teach Omri a lesson.

B 9. Why does Little Bear give Omri his belt made of white beads?
- A. He gives Omri the belt to bring to art class.
- B. He gives Omri the belt as payment for his new wife.
- C. He gives Omri the belt to give to Boone.
- D. He gives Omri the belt as a peace offering.

B 10. What is special about the key Omri finds to lock the cupboard?
- A. The key was to his grandmother's jewel box. Omri's mother wears it on a ribbon around her neck to keep it safe.
- B. The key was to his great-grandmother's jewel box. Omri's mother had worn it around her neck until the ribbon broke, and she almost lost it.
- C. The key was to his grandfather's safe. Omri's mother wears it on a chain around her neck to keep it from getting lost.
- D. The key was to his great-grandfather's desk. Omri's mother had worn it around her neck until the ribbon broke, and she almost lost it.

III. Vocabulary

O	1. COHERENT	A.	Enraged
S	2. SCORN	B.	To fall ill again after seeming to have made a recovery
E	3. LITHELY	C.	Replied in quick response to something someone has said
H	4. FOREBODING	D.	Immobile with fear
M	5. TOURNIQUET	E.	Bending easily
T	6. PENCE	F.	A thin rod or bar on which meat is pierced for broiling or roasting over a fire
N	7. HECTORING	G.	A euphoric state in which somebody is overwhelmed by happiness and unaware of anything else
F	8. SPIT	H.	A feeling that something bad is going to happen
D	9. PETRIFIED	I.	Open to physical danger or harm
A	10. INFURIATED	J.	Indebted to do something for someone
J	11. OBLIGED	K.	An agreed break in any type of dispute or feud
C	12. RETORTED	L.	Extremely small
K	13. TRUCE	M.	A tight band applied around an arm or a leg to stop bleeding
P	14. APPREHENSION	N.	Speaking in a domineering tone
L	15. MINUTE	O.	Logical
G	16. RAPTURE	P.	A feeling of anxiety or fear that something bad is going to occur
R	17. DISMAY	Q.	Puzzled
I	18. VULNERABLE	R.	To dishearten, alarm, cause loss of courage
B	19. RELAPSE	S.	A feeling of dislike
Q	20. BEMUSED	T.	Plural of penny

UNIT RESOURCE MATERIALS

BULLETIN BOARD IDEAS *The Indian in the Cupboard*

1. Save one corner of the board for the best of students' *The Indian in the Cupboard* writing assignments.

2. Take one of the word search puzzles from the extra activities packet and with a marker copy it over a large size on the bulletin board. Write the clue words to find to one side. Invite students prior to and after class to find the words and circle them on the bulletin board.

3. Write several of the most significant quotations from the book on the board on brightly colored paper.

4. Create a bulletin board listing the vocabulary words for this unit. As you complete sections of the novel and discuss the vocabulary for each section, write the definitions on the bulletin board. (If your board is one students face frequently, it will help them learn the words.)

5. Have students write down and illustrate their favorite similes and/or dialogue from the book.

6. Display a world map and have students locate the places where the characters lived.

7. Display the following quotation by Henry David Thoreau: "The language of friendship is not words but meanings." Reference it throughout the reading of the book, and have students discuss how it applies to the characters in the book.

8. Display a list of characteristics found in Native American myths and legends.

9. Draw a large cupboard. Have each student draw a toy he/she would place within the cupboard along with a description of why he/she would bring that toy to life.

MORE ACTIVITIES *The Indian in the Cupboard*

1. Have students work together to make a time line chronology of the events in the story. Take a large piece of construction paper and on one wall (or however you can physically arrange it in your room) place the events of the story along it. Students may want to add drawings or cut-out pictures to represent the events (as well as a written statement).

2. Have students design a book cover (front and back and inside flaps) for *The Indian in the Cupboard*.

3. Have students design a bulletin board (ready to be put up; not just sketched) for *The Indian in the Cupboard*.

4. Have students group the chapters together to show the larger structure of the novel. Have them explain why they chose the divisions they made.

5. Have students choose one part of the book (with sufficient dialogue) to rewrite as a play. In conjunction with this assignment, have students write a composition explaining the difficulties they encountered in changing from one written form to another.

6. Initiate a discussion of American Indian representation. Use the following questions to guide the discussion: How are American Indians represented today? What objects and practices do we associate with American Indian culture? What are some customs and traditions? Which term should be used, American Indian or Native American?

7. Have students research Native American games. Lacrosse is rich with tradition and Iroquois culture. *Lacrosse: the National Game of the Iroquois* by Diane Hoyt-Goldsmith presents the game's history along with information about the sport.

8. Research various Native American homes including: the igloo, the plank house, the pueblo, the tipi, and the wickiup. Have students compare and contrast them to the longhouse. Students can also make models of the homes for comparison.

9. Compare the film version of *The Indian in the Cupboard* to the book. How are key events portrayed in the movie version? How are the characters portrayed? Discuss similarities and differences. Do students prefer the movie or the book? Why?

UNIT WORD LIST *The Indian in the Cupboard*

No.	Word	Clue/Definition
1.	ADIEL	Omri's brother with the missing football shorts
2.	APRIL	Girl who teases Patrick at school
3.	ARROW	Little Bear removes this from Boone's chest.
4.	ART	Boone's best subject in school
5.	BANDAGE	What Omri needs from the medical orderly
6.	BEAR	Indian in the cupboard: Little ____
7.	BEARD	Slang for "I don't believe you."
8.	BEEF	Omri gave Little Bear canned _____ for breakfast.
9.	BELT	Little Bear gave Omri this as payment for his wife.
10.	BLOOD	Little Bear and Omri; Little Bear and Boone are _____ Brothers
11.	BOOHOO	Boone's nickname
12.	BOONE	Plastic cowboy who comes to life
13.	BOW	Belonged to the dead Indian chief
14.	CHAIN	Omri's mother plans to keep the key on this
15.	CHIEF	He died inside the cupboard: Indian _____.
16.	COKE	Drink Omri gave the Indian
17.	COWBOY	Omri was afraid Little Bear would kill him.
18.	CRIES	Reason for Boone's nickname
19.	CUPBOARD	Place where toys come to life
20.	DREAM	The soldier thinks Omri is a _____.
21.	EGG	Used as a wash basin for Boone & Little Bear: _____ cup
22.	GILLON	Omri's brother who gave Omri the cupboard
23.	HAIL	It was the size of a football to Little Bear and Boone.
24.	HALLUCY	Boone's nickname for Omri: _____-Nation
25.	HEADDRESS	Little Bear destroys this
26.	INDIAN	Patrick's birthday gift to Omri: Plastic _____
27.	IROQUOIS	Little Bear belonged to this tribe.
28.	JOHNSON	The headmaster: Mr. _____
29.	KEY	Used to open Omri's great-grandmother's jewel box
30.	KNIGHT	Source of the battle-ax
31.	KNOT	Cowboy escapes from the dress-up crate through this
32.	LONGHOUSE	Iroquois house
33.	NATIONS	Iroquois Indians were sometimes called this: The Five _____.
34.	PATRICK	Omri's friend
35.	PENICILLIN	Not yet discovered in Tommy's time.
36.	PICTURES	Little Bear criticized Omri's tepee because it lacked these.
37.	PLASTIC	Type of toys that become real in the cupboard.
38.	RAT	It was nesting in the floor under Omri's bed.

No.	Word	Clue/Definition
39.	SCALPS	Little Bear took thirty of these.
40.	SEED	Little Bear builds his longhouse in the _____ tray.
41.	SHORTS	What Adiel accuses Omri of stealing.
42.	SHOTS	This wakes Omri up at dawn.
43.	SISTERS	Maize, beans, and squash: 3 _____
44.	SKATEBOARD	Omri's birthday gift from his parents
45.	SOLDIER	He believed Omri was a character in a dream.
46.	SPIT	Little Bear cooks on this made from an erector set.
47.	STARS	Little Bear's wife: Bright ____
48.	STEALING	Mr. Yapp accused Omri of this.
49.	TEPEE	Where Little Bear sleeps his first night alive
50.	TOMMY	First World War soldier
51.	TRAIL	Book Omri reads about Indians: *On the _____ of the Iroquois*
52.	TRUTH	What Patrick tells Mr. Johnson
53.	WIFE	If Omri got him this, Little Bear would dance.
54.	YAPP	Owner of the store where Omri purchased plastic figures

WORD SEARCH - The Indian in the Cupboard

```
S T E A L I N G G E P B N R C B O O N E
K J F B E O S T G J E L A Q H R O A T G
A H Y Q I V N F O L F O T L A L I W I P
T W K J D B D G T M W O I K I D K E P P
E P I Y A A A R H T M D O C N D E E S M
B Z L F P R Y N E O R Y N I H P V O H J
O T R F E R R W D A U A S G E I L S O N
A R T C S O M N O A M S I T Q D E H R X
R Y P R X W O B H G G R E L I S B F T L
D S A G R S P P G I P E K E N P P G S Y
H T T J N U F A X L R T R V B E K X C C
S Z Y H C K P T R L A S L S N T R U T H
X M O Q D V N R L O P I M I L K L B B X
W J L F R Z W I Q N R S C Y D L B E E F
Y O B W O C W C G G I I S R A B T S G C
S X M O X C O K E H L I A H Y A P P Y P
G B H R O J N V N L T E P J O L B E A R
N T D Q G H M Q I O B Z X G A T K R Q N
Q X S R Y K O N H R T J M C D C S A R K
D J I R O Q U O I S Q C S P L A S T I C
```

Belonged to the dead Indian chief (3)
Book Omri reads about Indians: On the _____ of the Iroquois (5)
Boone's best subject in school (3)
Boone's nickname (6)
Boone's nickname for Omri:_____-Nation (7)
Cowboy escapes from the dress-up crate through this (4)
Drink Omri gave the Indian (4)
First World War soldier (5)
Girl who teases Patrick at school (5)
He believed Omri was a character in a dream. (7)
He died inside the cupboard: Indian _____. (5)
If Omri got him this, Little Bear would dance. (4)
Indian in the cupboard: Little _____ (4)
Iroquois Indians were sometimes called this: The Five _____. (7)
Iroquois house (9)
It was nesting in the floor under Omri's bed. (3)
It was the size of a football to Little Bear and Boone. (4)
Little Bear and Omri; Little Bear and Boone are _____ Brothers (5)
Little Bear belonged to this tribe. (8)
Little Bear builds his longhouse in the _____ tray. (4)
Little Bear cooks on this made from an erector set. (4)
Little Bear gave Omri this as payment for his wife. (4)
Little Bear removes this from Boone's chest. (5)
Little Bear took thirty of these. (6)

Maize, beans, and squash: 3 _____ (7)
Mr. Yapp accused Omri of this. (8)
Not yet discovered in Tommy's time. (10)
Omri gave Little Bear canned _____ for breakfast. (4)
Omri was afraid Little Bear would kill him. (6)
Omri's birthday gift from his parents (10)
Omri's brother who gave Omri the cupboard (6)
Omri's brother with the missing football shorts (5)
Omri's friend (7)
Omri's mother plans to keep the key on this (5)
Owner of the store where Omri purchased plastic figures (4)
Patrick's birthday gift to Omri: Plastic _____ (6)
Place where toys come to life (8)
Plastic cowboy who comes to life (5)
Reason for Boone's nickname (5)
Slang for (5)
Source of the battle-ax (6)
The headmaster: Mr. _____ (7)
The soldier thinks Omri is a _____. (5)
This wakes Omri up at dawn. (5)
Type of toys that become real in the cupboard. (7)
Used as a wash basin for Boone & Little Bear: _____ cup (3)
Used to open Omri's great-grandmother's jewel box (3)
What Adiel accuses Omri of stealing. (6)
What Omri needs from the medical orderly (7)
What Patrick tells Mr. Johnson (5)
Where Little Bear sleeps his first night alive (5)

WORD SEARCH ANSWER KEY - The Indian in the Cupboard

```
S T E A L I N G G E     B N     C B O O N E
K       E   T       E L A       H R O A T
A       I N O L     O T   A     I W I
T W   D B D G T M   O I   I D E P
E I   A A A R H T M D O C N D E E S
B   F R   N E O R Y N I H P   O H
O   E R     D A U A S   E I L   O
A R T   S O   N O A M S I T   D E   R
R   R   W O B   G G R E L I     F T
D A   S P P   I   E E     P S Y
  T     N U   A L   T R   E   C
S     H C K   T   L A S     N T R U T H
      O     N R   O P I   I   L
      J     I   N R S C   D L B E E F
Y O B W O C   C G   I I S R A   S
        O   C O K E H L I A H Y A P P Y
          O       N L T E     O L B E A R
            H     I O B     A T K R
              O N         T   C   S A
        I R O Q U O I S       S P L A S T I C
```

Belonged to the dead Indian chief (3)
Book Omri reads about Indians: On the _____ of the Iroquois (5)
Boone's best subject in school (3)
Boone's nickname (6)
Boone's nickname for Omri: _____-Nation (7)
Cowboy escapes from the dress-up crate through this (4)
Drink Omri gave the Indian (4)
First World War soldier (5)
Girl who teases Patrick at school (5)
He believed Omri was a character in a dream. (7)
He died inside the cupboard: Indian _____. (5)
If Omri got him this, Little Bear would dance. (4)
Indian in the cupboard: Little _____ (4)
Iroquois Indians were sometimes called this: The Five _____. (7)
Iroquois house (9)
It was nesting in the floor under Omri's bed. (3)
It was the size of a football to Little Bear and Boone. (4)
Little Bear and Omri; Little Bear and Boone are _____ Brothers (5)
Little Bear belonged to this tribe. (8)
Little Bear builds his longhouse in the _____ tray. (4)
Little Bear cooks on this made from an erector set. (4)
Little Bear gave Omri this as payment for his wife. (4)
Little Bear removes this from Boone's chest. (5)
Little Bear took thirty of these. (6)

Maize, beans, and squash: 3 _____ (7)
Mr. Yapp accused Omri of this. (8)
Not yet discovered in Tommy's time. (10)
Omri gave Little Bear canned _____ for breakfast. (4)
Omri was afraid Little Bear would kill him. (6)
Omri's birthday gift from his parents (10)
Omri's brother who gave Omri the cupboard (6)
Omri's brother with the missing football shorts (5)
Omri's friend (7)
Omri's mother plans to keep the key on this (5)
Owner of the store where Omri purchased plastic figures (4)
Patrick's birthday gift to Omri: Plastic _____ (6)
Place where toys come to life (8)
Plastic cowboy who comes to life (5)
Reason for Boone's nickname (5)
Slang for (5)
Source of the battle-ax (6)
The headmaster: Mr. _____ (7)
The soldier thinks Omri is a _____. (5)
This wakes Omri up at dawn. (5)
Type of toys that become real in the cupboard. (7)
Used as a wash basin for Boone & Little Bear: _____ cup (3)
Used to open Omri's great-grandmother's jewel box (3)
What Adiel accuses Omri of stealing. (6)
What Omri needs from the medical orderly (7)
What Patrick tells Mr. Johnson (5)
Where Little Bear sleeps his first night alive (5)

CROSSWORD - The Indian in the Cupboard

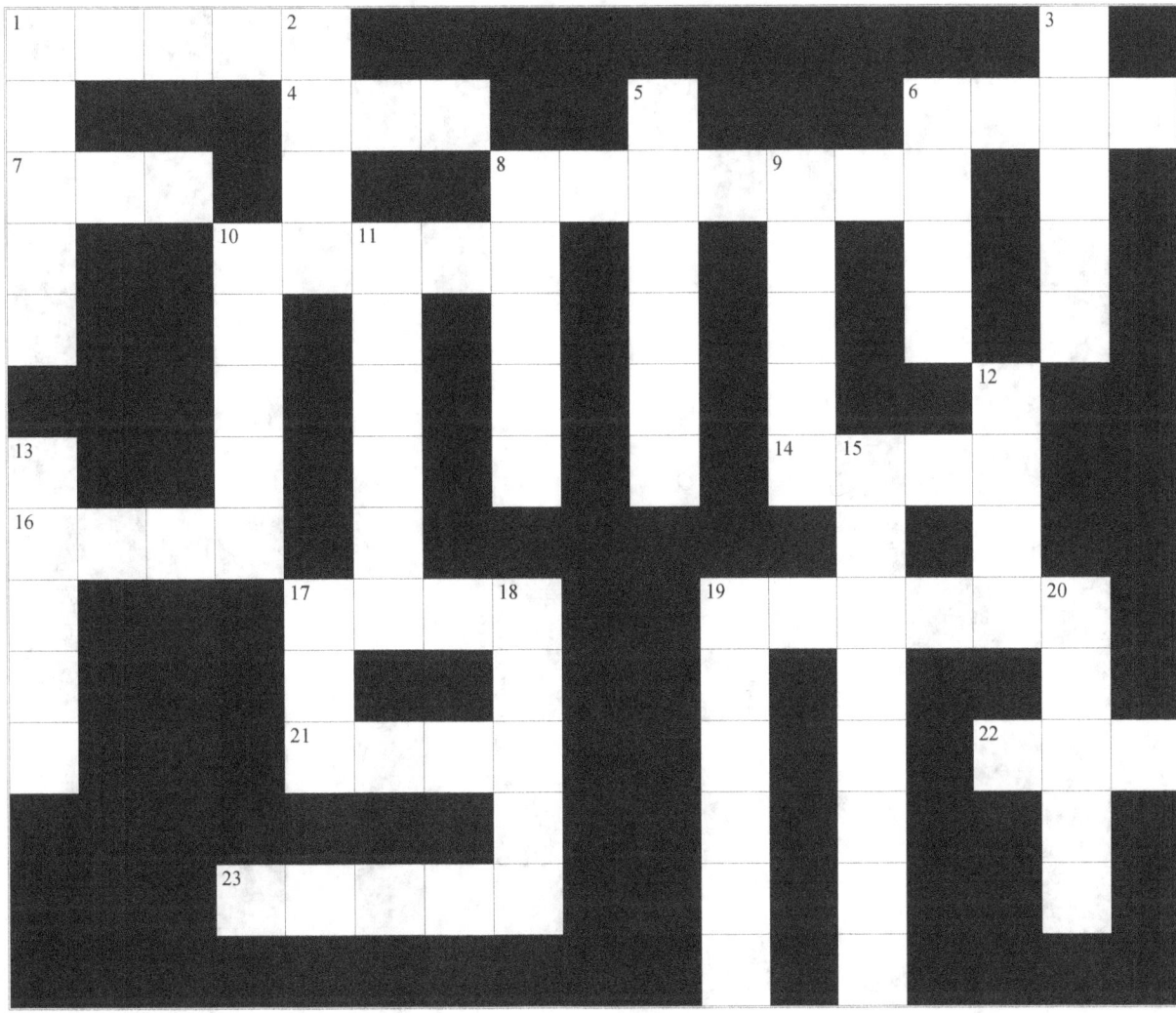

Across
1. Reason for Boone's nickname
4. Used as a wash basin for Boone & Little Bear: _____ cup
6. Omri gave Little Bear canned _____ for breakfast.
7. Boone's best subject in school
8. What Omri needs from the medical orderly
10. Omri's brother with the missing football shorts
14. If Omri got him this, Little Bear would dance.
16. It was the size of a football to Little Bear and Boone.
17. Cowboy escapes from the dress-up crate through this
19. What Adiel accuses Omri of stealing.
21. Owner of the store where Omri purchased plastic figures
22. Belonged to the dead Indian chief
23. Plastic cowboy who comes to life

Down
1. Omri's mother plans to keep the key on this
2. Little Bear builds his longhouse in the _____ tray.
3. Slang for
5. Source of the battle-ax
6. Indian in the cupboard: Little ____
8. Little Bear and Omri; Little Bear and Boone are _____ Brothers
9. Little Bear removes this from Boone's chest.
10. Girl who teases Patrick at school
11. Patrick's birthday gift to Omri: Plastic _____
12. Little Bear gave Omri this as payment for his wife.
13. He died inside the cupboard: Indian _____.
15. Little Bear belonged to this tribe.
17. Used to open Omri's great-grandmother's jewel box
18. Where Little Bear sleeps his first night alive
19. Little Bear took thirty of these.
20. This wakes Omri up at dawn.

CROSSWORD ANSWER KEY - The Indian in the Cupboard

	1 C	R	I	2 E	S							3 B	
	H			4 E	G	G		5 K			6 B	E	E	F
7 A	R	T		E			8 B	A	N	D	9 A	G	E		A
	I		10 A	D	11 I	E	L		I		R		A		R
	N		P		N		O		G		R		R		D
			R		D		O		H		O		12 B		
13 C			I		I		D		T		14 W	15 I	F	E	
16 H	A	I	L		A						R		L		
I				17 K	N	O	18 T		19 S	H	O	R	T	20 S
E				E			E		C		Q			H
F				21 Y	A	P	P		A		U		22 B	O	W
							E		L		O			T
				23 B	O	O	N	E		P		I		S
										S		S		

Across
1. Reason for Boone's nickname
4. Used as a wash basin for Boone & Little Bear: _____ cup
6. Omri gave Little Bear canned _____ for breakfast.
7. Boone's best subject in school
8. What Omri needs from the medical orderly
10. Omri's brother with the missing football shorts
14. If Omri got him this, Little Bear would dance.
16. It was the size of a football to Little Bear and Boone.
17. Cowboy escapes from the dress-up crate through this
19. What Adiel accuses Omri of stealing.
21. Owner of the store where Omri purchased plastic figures
22. Belonged to the dead Indian chief
23. Plastic cowboy who comes to life

Down
1. Omri's mother plans to keep the key on this
2. Little Bear builds his longhouse in the _____ tray.
3. Slang for
5. Source of the battle-ax
6. Indian in the cupboard: Little ____
8. Little Bear and Omri; Little Bear and Boone are _____ Brothers
9. Little Bear removes this from Boone's chest.
10. Girl who teases Patrick at school
11. Patrick's birthday gift to Omri: Plastic _____
12. Little Bear gave Omri this as payment for his wife.
13. He died inside the cupboard: Indian _____.
15. Little Bear belonged to this tribe.
17. Used to open Omri's great-grandmother's jewel box
18. Where Little Bear sleeps his first night alive
19. Little Bear took thirty of these.
20. This wakes Omri up at dawn.

Matching Worksheet 1 *The Indian in the Cupboard*

____ 1. PATRICK   A. Drink Omri gave the Indian
____ 2. COKE   B. Omri's friend
____ 3. IROQUOIS   C. Used to open Omri's great-grandmother's jewel box
____ 4. PICTURES   D. Little Bear belonged to this tribe.
____ 5. BELT   E. Patrick's birthday gift to Omri: Plastic _____
____ 6. KNIGHT   F. Source of the battle-ax
____ 7. WIFE   G. It was the size of a football to Little Bear and Boone.
____ 8. HAIL   H. Boone's nickname
____ 9. ART   I. Maize, beans, and squash: 3 _____
____ 10. INDIAN   J. If Omri got him this, Little Bear would dance.
____ 11. BEARD   K. Little Bear criticized Omri's tepee because it lacked these.
____ 12. NATIONS   L. Boone's best subject in school
____ 13. TRAIL   M. Slang for "I don't believe you."
____ 14. JOHNSON   N. Omri's brother with the missing football shorts
____ 15. BOOHOO   O. Little Bear gave Omri this as payment for his wife.
____ 16. SISTERS   P. Iroquois house
____ 17. LONGHOUSE   Q. The headmaster: Mr. _____
____ 18. ADIEL   R. Iroquois Indians were sometimes called this: The Five _____.
____ 19. BEAR   S. Indian in the cupboard: Little ____
____ 20. KEY   T. Book Omri reads about Indians: *On the _____ of the Iroquois*

Matching Worksheet 1 ANSWER KEY *The Indian in the Cupboard*

B	1.	PATRICK	A.	Drink Omri gave the Indian
A	2.	COKE	B.	Omri's friend
D	3.	IROQUOIS	C.	Used to open Omri's great-grandmother's jewel box
K	4.	PICTURES	D.	Little Bear belonged to this tribe.
O	5.	BELT	E.	Patrick's birthday gift to Omri: Plastic _____
F	6.	KNIGHT	F.	Source of the battle-ax
J	7.	WIFE	G.	It was the size of a football to Little Bear and Boone.
G	8.	HAIL	H.	Boone's nickname
L	9.	ART	I.	Maize, beans, and squash: 3 _____
E	10.	INDIAN	J.	If Omri got him this, Little Bear would dance.
M	11.	BEARD	K.	Little Bear criticized Omri's tepee because it lacked these.
R	12.	NATIONS	L.	Boone's best subject in school
T	13.	TRAIL	M.	Slang for "I don't believe you."
Q	14.	JOHNSON	N.	Omri's brother with the missing football shorts
H	15.	BOOHOO	O.	Little Bear gave Omri this as payment for his wife.
I	16.	SISTERS	P.	Iroquois house
P	17.	LONGHOUSE	Q.	The headmaster: Mr. _____
N	18.	ADIEL	R.	Iroquois Indians were sometimes called this: The Five _____.
S	19.	BEAR	S.	Indian in the cupboard: Little ____
C	20.	KEY	T.	Book Omri reads about Indians: *On the _____ of the Iroquois*

Matching Worksheet 2 *The Indian in the Cupboard*

____ 1. STEALING   A. Little Bear belonged to this tribe.
____ 2. TOMMY   B. It was the size of a football to Little Bear and Boone.
____ 3. LONGHOUSE   C. Drink Omri gave the Indian
____ 4. TRUTH   D. He believed Omri was a character in a dream.
____ 5. YAPP   E. Girl who teases Patrick at school
____ 6. BOOHOO   F. Boone's nickname
____ 7. JOHNSON   G. Omri was afraid Little Bear would kill him.
____ 8. CHIEF   H. He died inside the cupboard: Indian _____.
____ 9. SKATEBOARD   I. Iroquois house
____ 10. STARS   J. First World War soldier
____ 11. APRIL   K. Omri's brother who gave Omri the cupboard
____ 12. HAIL   L. Little Bear's wife: Bright ____
____ 13. COWBOY   M. Mr. Yapp accused Omri of this.
____ 14. SOLDIER   N. Owner of the store where Omri purchased plastic figures
____ 15. BEEF   O. What Patrick tells Mr. Johnson
____ 16. IROQUOIS   P. Omri's birthday gift from his parents
____ 17. COKE   Q. The headmaster: Mr. _____
____ 18. CUPBOARD   R. Omri gave Little Bear canned _____ for breakfast.
____ 19. BOONE   S. Place where toys come to life
____ 20. GILLON   T. Plastic cowboy who comes to life

Matching Worksheet 2 ANSWER KEY *The Indian in the Cupboard*

M	1.	STEALING	A.	Little Bear belonged to this tribe.
J	2.	TOMMY	B.	It was the size of a football to Little Bear and Boone.
I	3.	LONGHOUSE	C.	Drink Omri gave the Indian
O	4.	TRUTH	D.	He believed Omri was a character in a dream.
N	5.	YAPP	E.	Girl who teases Patrick at school
F	6.	BOOHOO	F.	Boone's nickname
Q	7.	JOHNSON	G.	Omri was afraid Little Bear would kill him.
H	8.	CHIEF	H.	He died inside the cupboard: Indian _____.
P	9.	SKATEBOARD	I.	Iroquois house
L	10.	STARS	J.	First World War soldier
E	11.	APRIL	K.	Omri's brother who gave Omri the cupboard
B	12.	HAIL	L.	Little Bear's wife: Bright _____
G	13.	COWBOY	M.	Mr. Yapp accused Omri of this.
D	14.	SOLDIER	N.	Owner of the store where Omri purchased plastic figures
R	15.	BEEF	O.	What Patrick tells Mr. Johnson
A	16.	IROQUOIS	P.	Omri's birthday gift from his parents
C	17.	COKE	Q.	The headmaster: Mr. _____
S	18.	CUPBOARD	R.	Omri gave Little Bear canned _____ for breakfast.
T	19.	BOONE	S.	Place where toys come to life
K	20.	GILLON	T.	Plastic cowboy who comes to life

Juggle Letter Worksheet 1 *The Indian in the Cupboard*

_____ = 1. LGTAEISN
Mr. Yapp accused Omri of this.

_____ = 2. GILNLO
Omri's brother who gave Omri the cupboard

_____ = 3. TASNNIO
Iroquois Indians were sometimes called this: The Five _____.

_____ = 4. IALTR
Book Omri reads about Indians: *On the _____ of the Iroquois*

_____ = 5. OJSNNOH
The headmaster: Mr. _____

_____ = 6. OOHBOO
Boone's nickname

_____ = 7. RITSSES
Maize, beans, and squash: 3 _____

_____ = 8. NLGUOOSHE
Iroquois house

_____ = 9. BDREA
Slang for "I don't believe you."

_____ = 10. RBUOADPC
Place where toys come to life

_____ = 11. IUSOORIQ
Little Bear belonged to this tribe.

_____ = 12. OELDRIS
He believed Omri was a character in a dream.

_____ = 13. KHITNG
Source of the battle-ax

_____ = 14. BOYCOW
Omri was afraid Little Bear would kill him.

_____ = 15. RAPTKCI
Omri's friend

Juggle Letter Worksheet 1 ANSWER KEY *The Indian in the Cupboard*

STEALING	= 1.	LGTAEISN
		Mr. Yapp accused Omri of this.
GILLON	= 2.	GILNLO
		Omri's brother who gave Omri the cupboard
NATIONS	= 3.	TASNNIO
		Iroquois Indians were sometimes called this: The Five _____.
TRAIL	= 4.	IALTR
		Book Omri reads about Indians: *On the _____ of the Iroquois*
JOHNSON	= 5.	OJSNNOH
		The headmaster: Mr. _____
BOOHOO	= 6.	OOHBOO
		Boone's nickname
SISTERS	= 7.	RITSSES
		Maize, beans, and squash: 3 _____
LONGHOUSE	= 8.	NLGUOOSHE
		Iroquois house
BEARD	= 9.	BDREA
		Slang for "I don't believe you."
CUPBOARD	= 10.	RBUOADPC
		Place where toys come to life
IROQUOIS	= 11.	IUSOORIQ
		Little Bear belonged to this tribe.
SOLDIER	= 12.	OELDRIS
		He believed Omri was a character in a dream.
KNIGHT	= 13.	KHITNG
		Source of the battle-ax
COWBOY	= 14.	BOYCOW
		Omri was afraid Little Bear would kill him.
PATRICK	= 15.	RAPTKCI
		Omri's friend

Juggle Letter Worksheet 2 *The Indian in the Cupboard*

_____   = 1. NAILGEST
                         Mr. Yapp accused Omri of this.
_____   = 2. NSOAITN
                         Iroquois Indians were sometimes called this: The Five _____.
_____   = 3. ADRAEOTSBK
                         Omri's birthday gift from his parents
_____   = 4. ESTSIRS
                         Maize, beans, and squash: 3 _____
_____   = 5. OUNOHELSG
                         Iroquois house
_____   = 6. MMTYO
                         First World War soldier
_____   = 7. EDLIA
                         Omri's brother with the missing football shorts
_____   = 8. QUORISIO
                         Little Bear belonged to this tribe.
_____   = 9. UCPERIST
                         Little Bear criticized Omri's tepee because it lacked these.
_____   = 10. ODEISLR
                         He believed Omri was a character in a dream.
_____   = 11. GKTNHI
                         Source of the battle-ax
_____   = 12. CBOOYW
                         Omri was afraid Little Bear would kill him.
_____   = 13. EFIW
                         If Omri got him this, Little Bear would dance.
_____   = 14. ALIH
                         It was the size of a football to Little Bear and Boone.
_____   = 15. ILGLNO
                         Omri's brother who gave Omri the cupboard

Juggle Letter Worksheet 2 ANSWER KEY *The Indian in the Cupboard*

STEALING	= 1.	NAILGEST
		Mr. Yapp accused Omri of this.
NATIONS	= 2.	NSOAITN
		Iroquois Indians were sometimes called this: The Five _____.
SKATEBOARD	= 3.	ADRAEOTSBK
		Omri's birthday gift from his parents
SISTERS	= 4.	ESTSIRS
		Maize, beans, and squash: 3 _____
LONGHOUSE	= 5.	OUNOHELSG
		Iroquois house
TOMMY	= 6.	MMTYO
		First World War soldier
ADIEL	= 7.	EDLIA
		Omri's brother with the missing football shorts
IROQUOIS	= 8.	QUORISIO
		Little Bear belonged to this tribe.
PICTURES	= 9.	UCPERIST
		Little Bear criticized Omri's tepee because it lacked these.
SOLDIER	= 10.	ODEISLR
		He believed Omri was a character in a dream.
KNIGHT	= 11.	GKTNHI
		Source of the battle-ax
COWBOY	= 12.	CBOOYW
		Omri was afraid Little Bear would kill him.
WIFE	= 13.	EFIW
		If Omri got him this, Little Bear would dance.
HAIL	= 14.	ALIH
		It was the size of a football to Little Bear and Boone.
GILLON	= 15.	ILGLNO
		Omri's brother who gave Omri the cupboard

VOCABULARY RESOURCE MATERIALS

The Indian in the Cupboard Vocabulary

No.	Word	Clue/Definition
1.	AGHAST	Overcome with shock
2.	APPALLED	Shocked
3.	APPREHENSION	A feeling of anxiety or fear that something bad is going to occur
4.	BAFFLEMENT	Bewilderment
5.	BANDOLIER	A kind of belt worn over one shoulder and across the chest
6.	BEMUSED	Puzzled
7.	BRIDLE	A set of leather straps fitted to a horse's head that includes the bit and the reins
8.	COAXED	Persuaded gently
9.	COHERENT	Logical
10.	DEFIANT	Tending to confront and challenge
11.	DESPAIR	A feeling of hopelessness
12.	DISMAY	To dishearten, alarm, cause loss of courage
13.	FIENDISH	Devilish
14.	FLUMMOXED	Perplexed
15.	FOREBODING	A feeling that something bad is going to happen
16.	GALVANIZED	Stimulated into great activity
17.	GAPED	Stared in open-mouthed surprise
18.	HECTORING	Speaking in a domineering tone
19.	IMPERIOUSLY	Domineeringly
20.	INCREDULOUS	Unbelieving
21.	INFURIATED	Enraged
22.	INTRICATE	Containing many details or small parts that are skillfully made
23.	JOISTS	Floor, roof, or ceiling supports
24.	LITHELY	Bending easily
25.	LONGHOUSE	A long, bark-covered dwelling place built by some Native North American peoples, especially the Iroquois
26.	MAGNANIMOUSLY	Nobly
27.	MAIZE	Corn
28.	MINUTE	Extremely small
29.	MULISH	Unwilling to cooperate or listen to suggestions
30.	MYRIAD	Numerous
31.	OBLIGED	Indebted to do something for someone
32.	OMNIVOROUS	Eating any kind of food, including both plants and animals
33.	PEEVISHLY	Irritably
34.	PENCE	Plural of penny
35.	PERILS	Sources of potential harm

No.	Word	Clue/Definition
36.	PERSECUTOR	Oppressor; tyrant
37.	PETRIFIED	Immobile with fear
38.	RAUCOUS	Loud and hoarse or unpleasant-sounding
39.	RANSACKED	Searched thoroughly but handled carelessly
40.	RAPTURE	A euphoric state in which somebody is overwhelmed by happiness and unaware of anything else
41.	RAVENOUSLY	Hungrily
42.	REGRETFULLY	Remorsefully
43.	RELAPSE	To fall ill again after seeming to have made a recovery
44.	RELUCTANT	Hesitant
45.	RESTIVE	Having little patience and on the verge of resisting control
46.	RETORTED	Replied in quick response to something someone has said
47.	SAGEBRUSH	A bushy plant native to dry regions of North America with silvery wedge-shaped leaves and clusters of small white flowers
48.	SCALPS	The skin and hair covering the skulls of enemies; cut off as trophies
49.	SCORN	A feeling of dislike
50.	SEPTIC	Full of pus
51.	SNIDE	Sarcastic
52.	SPIT	A thin rod or bar on which meat is pierced for broiling or roasting over a fire
53.	TACTICS	A course of action to achieve short-term gains
54.	TETHERED	Tied with a rope or chain
55.	TOURNIQUET	A tight band applied around an arm or a leg to stop bleeding
56.	TRANSFIXED	Made motionless
57.	TRANSFUSION	The transfer of blood into the bloodstream of somebody who has lost blood
58.	TRUCE	An agreed break in any type of dispute or feud
59.	UNCOMPROMISINGLY	Unwilling to back down
60.	UNWARILY	Not cautiously
61.	VULNERABLE	Open to physical danger or harm

VOCABULARY WORD SEARCH - The Indian in the Cupboard

```
S E P T I C B T R A N S F U S I O N M Q
T C F N S S R A R S P B C G X T B U I C
S Q A H F W I E N A E P Q O Q G L R N J
I P D L F S D X L D N F A C R I I E U Z
O B E Q P P L M I A O S K L S N G T T F
J L S T C S E N E N P L F H L G E O E W
V M P X R P S R V F C S I I W E D R J C
U T A C T I C S I I I R E E X C D T K D
L E I I R B F L T L N E E Q R E T E L S
N T R S Z P F I S T S T N D S D D D F C
E H M K B E W T E R H R R D U P E N C E
R E S F A R Q H R D A H A I I L I F C Y
A R A F F S F E K L E P E U C S O T V J
B E G B F E J L M C G B T C C A H U T G
L D E E L C C Y U R W D O U T O T J S Z
E L B M E U J R V M E A Q J R O U E C K
G F R U M T T J Q P X I M G L E R S P Z
G S U S E O D S A E X R U N W A R I L Y
S Y S E N R J G D N H Y A G H A S T N L
F H H D T N A I F E D M C D I S M A Y G
```

A set of leather straps fitted to a horse's head that includes the bit and the reins (6)
A course of action to achieve short-term gains (7)
A euphoric state in which somebody is overwhelmed by happiness and unaware of anything else (7)
A feeling of dislike (5)
A feeling of hopelessness (7)
A kind of belt worn over one shoulder and across the chest (9)
A thin rod or bar on which meat is pierced for broiling or roasting over a fire (4)
An agreed break in any type of dispute or feud (5)
Bending easily (7)
Bewilderment (10)
Containing many details or small parts that are skillfully made (9)
Corn (5)
Devilish (8)
Extremely small (6)
Floor, roof, or ceiling supports (6)
Full of pus (6)
Having little patience and on the verge of resisting control (7)
Immobile with fear (9)
Indebted to do something for someone (7)
Loud and hoarse or unpleasant-sounding (7)
Made motionless (10)

Numerous (6)
Open to physical danger or harm (10)
Oppressor; tyrant (10)
Overcome with shock (6)
Persuaded gently (6)
Plant native to North America with silvery wedge-shaped leaves and clusters of small white flowers (
Plural of penny (5)
Puzzled (7)
Replied in quick response to something someone has said (8)
Sarcastic (5)
Shocked (8)
Sources of potential harm (6)
Speaking in a domineering tone (9)
Stared in open-mouthed surprise (5)
Tending to confront and challenge (7)
The skin and hair covering the skulls of enemies; cut off as trophies (6)
The transfer of blood into the bloodstream of somebody who has lost blood (11)
Tied with a rope or chain (8)
To dishearten, alarm, cause loss of courage (6)
To fall ill again after seeming to have made a recovery (7)
Unbelieving (11)

VOCABULARY WORD SEARCH ANSWER KEY- The Indian in the Cupboard

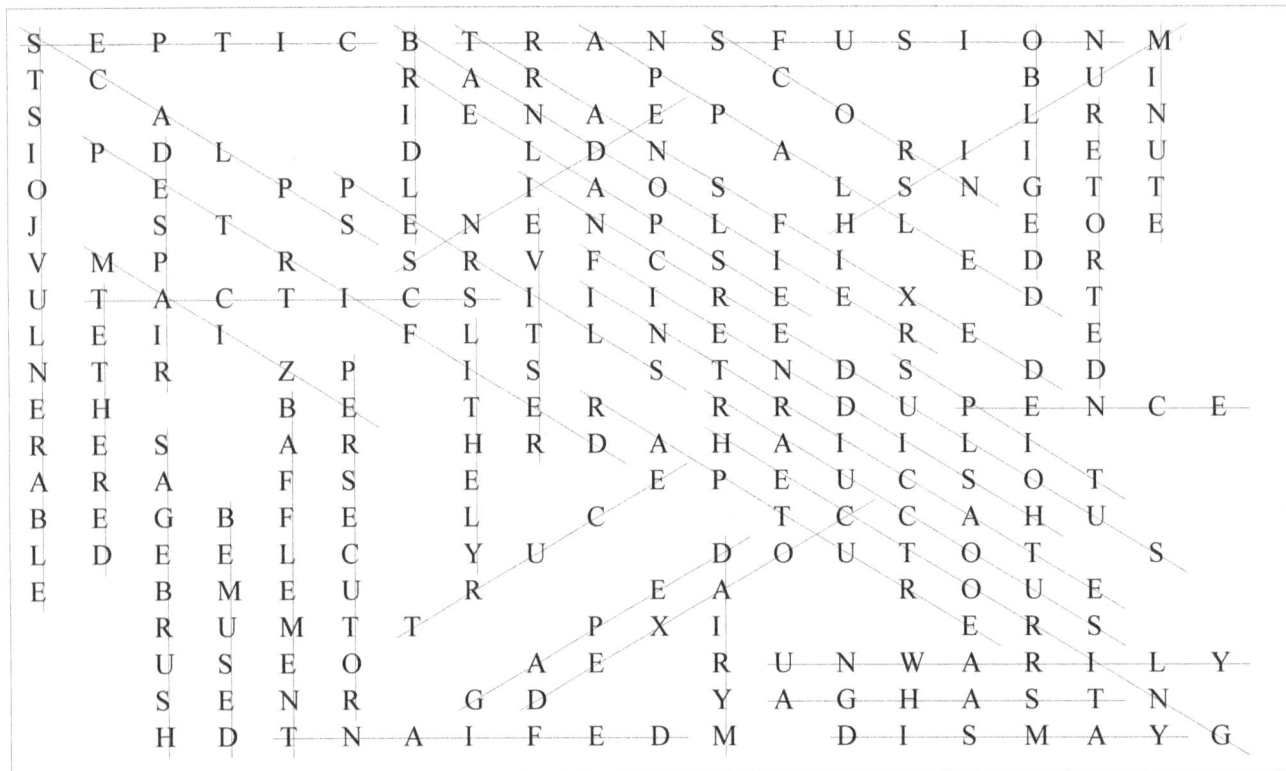

A set of leather straps fitted to a horse's head that includes the bit and the reins (6)
A course of action to achieve short-term gains (7)
A euphoric state in which somebody is overwhelmed by happiness and unaware of anything else (7)
A feeling of dislike (5)
A feeling of hopelessness (7)
A kind of belt worn over one shoulder and across the chest (9)
A thin rod or bar on which meat is pierced for broiling or roasting over a fire (4)
An agreed break in any type of dispute or feud (5)
Bending easily (7)
Bewilderment (10)
Containing many details or small parts that are skillfully made (9)
Corn (5)
Devilish (8)
Extremely small (6)
Floor, roof, or ceiling supports (6)
Full of pus (6)
Having little patience and on the verge of resisting control (7)
Immobile with fear (9)
Indebted to do something for someone (7)
Loud and hoarse or unpleasant-sounding (7)
Made motionless (10)

Numerous (6)
Open to physical danger or harm (10)
Oppressor; tyrant (10)
Overcome with shock (6)
Persuaded gently (6)
Plant native to North America with silvery wedge-shaped leaves and clusters of small white flowers (
Plural of penny (5)
Puzzled (7)
Replied in quick response to something someone has said (8)
Sarcastic (5)
Shocked (8)
Sources of potential harm (6)
Speaking in a domineering tone (9)
Stared in open-mouthed surprise (5)
Tending to confront and challenge (7)
The skin and hair covering the skulls of enemies; cut off as trophies (6)
The transfer of blood into the bloodstream of somebody who has lost blood (11)
Tied with a rope or chain (8)
To dishearten, alarm, cause loss of courage (6)
To fall ill again after seeming to have made a recovery (7)
Unbelieving (11)

VOCABULARY CROSSWORD - The Indian in the Cupboard

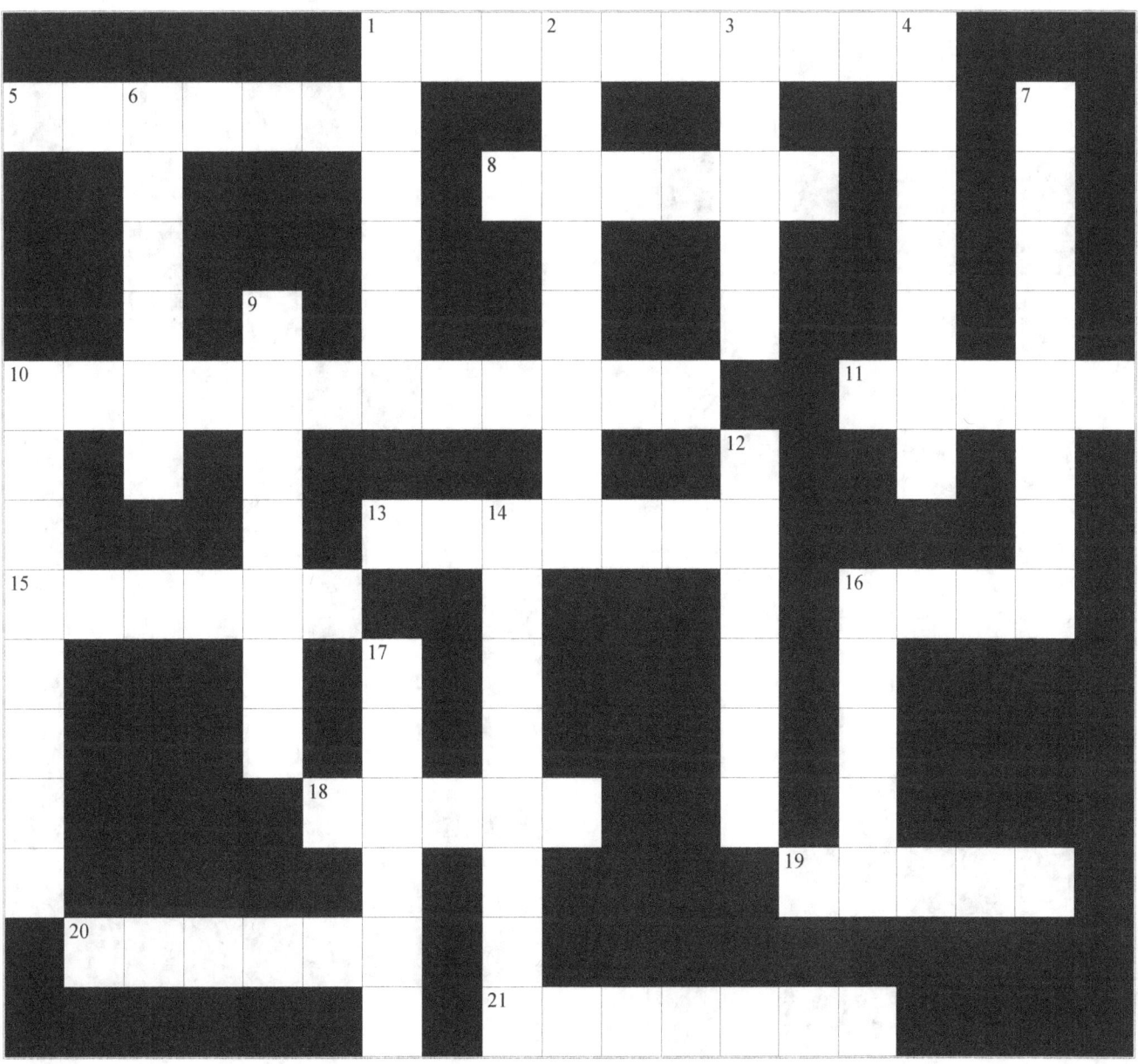

Across
1. Bewilderment
5. A feeling of hopelessness
8. Full of pus
10. A feeling of anxiety or fear that something bad is going to occur
11. A feeling of dislike
13. Bending easily
15. Overcome with shock
16. A thin rod or bar on which meat is pierced for broiling or roasting over a fire
18. Stared in open-mouthed surprise
19. Plural of penny
20. Extremely small
21. Tending to confront and challenge

Down
1. A set of leather straps fitted to a horse's head that includes the bit and the reins
2. Devilish
3. Corn
4. A course of action to achieve short-term gains
6. The skin and hair covering the skulls of enemies; cut off as trophies
7. Logical
9. Puzzled
10. Shocked
12. Numerous
14. Tied with a rope or chain
16. Sarcastic
17. Persuaded gently

VOCABULARY CROSSWORD ANSWER KEY - The Indian in the Cupboard

Across
1. Bewilderment
5. A feeling of hopelessness
8. Full of pus
10. A feeling of anxiety or fear that something bad is going to occur
11. A feeling of dislike
13. Bending easily
15. Overcome with shock
16. A thin rod or bar on which meat is pierced for broiling or roasting over a fire
18. Stared in open-mouthed surprise
19. Plural of penny
20. Extremely small
21. Tending to confront and challenge

Down
1. A set of leather straps fitted to a horse's head that includes the bit and the reins
2. Devilish
3. Corn
4. A course of action to achieve short-term gains
6. The skin and hair covering the skulls of enemies; cut off as trophies
7. Logical
9. Puzzled
10. Shocked
12. Numerous
14. Tied with a rope or chain
16. Sarcastic
17. Persuaded gently

Vocab Matching Worksheet 1 *The Indian in the Cupboard*

____ 1. PERILS   A. To dishearten, alarm, cause loss of courage

____ 2. DEFIANT   B. A set of leather straps fitted to a horse's head that includes the bit and the reins

____ 3. BRIDLE   C. Speaking in a domineering tone

____ 4. BEMUSED   D. Unwilling to cooperate or listen to suggestions

____ 5. BANDOLIER   E. Sources of potential harm

____ 6. APPALLED   F. Stared in open-mouthed surprise

____ 7. HECTORING   G. Tending to confront and challenge

____ 8. GAPED   H. Irritably

____ 9. FLUMMOXED   I. Bending easily

____ 10. DISMAY   J. Numerous

____ 11. INCREDULOUS   K. Nobly

____ 12. PEEVISHLY   L. Perplexed

____ 13. OBLIGED   M. Indebted to do something for someone

____ 14. MYRIAD   N. A kind of belt worn over one shoulder and across the chest

____ 15. MULISH   O. Unbelieving

____ 16. MINUTE   P. Extremely small

____ 17. MAGNANIMOUSLY   Q. Puzzled

____ 18. LITHELY   R. Shocked

____ 19. INTRICATE   S. Containing many details or small parts that are skillfully made

____ 20. FIENDISH   T. Devilish

Vocab Matching Worksheet 1 ANSWER KEY *The Indian in the Cupboard*

E	1.	PERILS	A.	To dishearten, alarm, cause loss of courage	
G	2.	DEFIANT	B.	A set of leather straps fitted to a horse's head that includes the bit and the reins	
B	3.	BRIDLE	C.	Speaking in a domineering tone	
Q	4.	BEMUSED	D.	Unwilling to cooperate or listen to suggestions	
N	5.	BANDOLIER	E.	Sources of potential harm	
R	6.	APPALLED	F.	Stared in open-mouthed surprise	
C	7.	HECTORING	G.	Tending to confront and challenge	
F	8.	GAPED	H.	Irritably	
L	9.	FLUMMOXED	I.	Bending easily	
A	10.	DISMAY	J.	Numerous	
O	11.	INCREDULOUS	K.	Nobly	
H	12.	PEEVISHLY	L.	Perplexed	
M	13.	OBLIGED	M.	Indebted to do something for someone	
J	14.	MYRIAD	N.	A kind of belt worn over one shoulder and across the chest	
D	15.	MULISH	O.	Unbelieving	
P	16.	MINUTE	P.	Extremely small	
K	17.	MAGNANIMOUSLY	Q.	Puzzled	
I	18.	LITHELY	R.	Shocked	
S	19.	INTRICATE	S.	Containing many details or small parts that are skillfully made	
T	20.	FIENDISH	T.	Devilish	

Vocab Matching Worksheet 2 *The Indian in the Cupboard*

____ 1. VULNERABLE   A. Open to physical danger or harm

____ 2. RAVENOUSLY   B. A thin rod or bar on which meat is pierced for broiling or roasting over a fire

____ 3. RAPTURE   C. Hungrily

____ 4. RANSACKED   D. An agreed break in any type of dispute or feud

____ 5. PETRIFIED   E. Unwilling to cooperate or listen to suggestions

____ 6. PERILS   F. Made motionless

____ 7. OBLIGED   G. Full of pus

____ 8. MULISH   H. Not cautiously

____ 9. LITHELY   I. Immobile with fear

____ 10. RELAPSE   J. Indebted to do something for someone

____ 11. RESTIVE   K. Speaking in a domineering tone

____ 12. UNWARILY   L. A euphoric state in which somebody is overwhelmed by happiness and unaware of anything else

____ 13. TRUCE   M. Sources of potential harm

____ 14. TRANSFIXED   N. To fall ill again after seeming to have made a recovery

____ 15. TETHERED   O. Searched thoroughly but handled carelessly

____ 16. SPIT   P. Replied in quick response to something someone has said

____ 17. SEPTIC   Q. A feeling of dislike

____ 18. SCORN   R. Bending easily

____ 19. RETORTED   S. Having little patience and on the verge of resisting control

____ 20. HECTORING   T. Tied with a rope or chain

Vocab Matching Worksheet 2 ANSWER KEY *The Indian in the Cupboard*

A	1.	VULNERABLE	A.	Open to physical danger or harm
C	2.	RAVENOUSLY	B.	A thin rod or bar on which meat is pierced for broiling or roasting over a fire
L	3.	RAPTURE	C.	Hungrily
O	4.	RANSACKED	D.	An agreed break in any type of dispute or feud
I	5.	PETRIFIED	E.	Unwilling to cooperate or listen to suggestions
M	6.	PERILS	F.	Made motionless
J	7.	OBLIGED	G.	Full of pus
E	8.	MULISH	H.	Not cautiously
R	9.	LITHELY	I.	Immobile with fear
N	10.	RELAPSE	J.	Indebted to do something for someone
S	11.	RESTIVE	K.	Speaking in a domineering tone
H	12.	UNWARILY	L.	A euphoric state in which somebody is overwhelmed by happiness and unaware of anything else
D	13.	TRUCE	M.	Sources of potential harm
F	14.	TRANSFIXED	N.	To fall ill again after seeming to have made a recovery
T	15.	TETHERED	O.	Searched thoroughly but handled carelessly
B	16.	SPIT	P.	Replied in quick response to something someone has said
G	17.	SEPTIC	Q.	A feeling of dislike
Q	18.	SCORN	R.	Bending easily
P	19.	RETORTED	S.	Having little patience and on the verge of resisting control
K	20.	HECTORING	T.	Tied with a rope or chain

Vocab Juggle Letter Worksheet 1 *The Indian in the Cupboard*

_____ = 1. EDTOTRER
Replied in quick response to something someone has said

_____ = 2. HGAATS
Overcome with shock

_____ = 3. UMBEESD
Puzzled

_____ = 4. EDOAXC
Persuaded gently

_____ = 5. FTDINAE
Tending to confront and challenge

_____ = 6. IAVLZADEGN
Stimulated into great activity

_____ = 7. ROHENCGIT
Speaking in a domineering tone

_____ = 8. AIEINCTRT
Containing many details or small parts that are skillfully made

_____ = 9. YEHLTLI
Bending easily

_____ = 10. MOIYNLSANAMGU
Nobly

_____ = 11. RIMYAD
Numerous

_____ = 12. SUIROVMOON
Eating any kind of food, including both plants and animals

_____ = 13. PEECN
Plural of penny

_____ = 14. CERUOSPTER
Oppressor; tyrant

_____ = 15. PNRLCUOYINMOIGMS
Unwilling to back down

Vocab Juggle Letter Worksheet 1 ANSWER KEY *The Indian in the Cupboard*

RETORTED	= 1.	EDTOTRER Replied in quick response to something someone has said
AGHAST	= 2.	HGAATS Overcome with shock
BEMUSED	= 3.	UMBEESD Puzzled
COAXED	= 4.	EDOAXC Persuaded gently
DEFIANT	= 5.	FTDINAE Tending to confront and challenge
GALVANIZED	= 6.	IAVLZADEGN Stimulated into great activity
HECTORING	= 7.	ROHENCGIT Speaking in a domineering tone
INTRICATE	= 8.	AIEINCTRT Containing many details or small parts that are skillfully made
LITHELY	= 9.	YEHLTLI Bending easily
MAGNANIMOUSLY	= 10.	MOIYNLSANAMGU Nobly
MYRIAD	= 11.	RIMYAD Numerous
OMNIVOROUS	= 12.	SUIROVMOON Eating any kind of food, including both plants and animals
PENCE	= 13.	PEECN Plural of penny
PERSECUTOR	= 14.	CERUOSPTER Oppressor; tyrant
UNCOMPROMISINGLY	= 15.	PNRLCUOYINMOIGMS Unwilling to back down

Vocab Juggle Letter Worksheet 2 *The Indian in the Cupboard*

_____ = 1. ELBRUENALV
Open to physical danger or harm

_____ = 2. NVIZAALEDG
Stimulated into great activity

_____ = 3. JTIOSS
Floor, roof, or ceiling supports

_____ = 4. EUNIMT
Extremely small

_____ = 5. IREPIETFD
Immobile with fear

_____ = 6. RLVUSEOAYN
Hungrily

_____ = 7. LRYGERTFELU
Remorsefully

_____ = 8. OERREDTT
Replied in quick response to something someone has said

_____ = 9. SPCLAS
The skin and hair covering the skulls of enemies; cut off as trophies

_____ = 10. EDISN
Sarcastic

_____ = 11. TPSI
A thin rod or bar on which meat is pierced for broiling or roasting over a fire

_____ = 12. ITCACST
A course of action to achieve short-term gains

_____ = 13. XAIENTSFDR
Made motionless

_____ = 14. MPUOLRCNONIIGMYS
Unwilling to back down

_____ = 15. FTBALNEMEF
Bewilderment

Vocab Juggle Letter Worksheet 2 ANSWER KEY *The Indian in the Cupboard*

VULNERABLE	= 1.	ELBRUENALV Open to physical danger or harm
GALVANIZED	= 2.	NVIZAALEDG Stimulated into great activity
JOISTS	= 3.	JTIOSS Floor, roof, or ceiling supports
MINUTE	= 4.	EUNIMT Extremely small
PETRIFIED	= 5.	IREPIETFD Immobile with fear
RAVENOUSLY	= 6.	RLVUSEOAYN Hungrily
REGRETFULLY	= 7.	LRYGERTFELU Remorsefully
RETORTED	= 8.	OERREDTT Replied in quick response to something someone has said
SCALPS	= 9.	SPCLAS The skin and hair covering the skulls of enemies; cut off as trophies
SNIDE	= 10.	EDISN Sarcastic
SPIT	= 11.	TPSI A thin rod or bar on which meat is pierced for broiling or roasting over a fire
TACTICS	= 12.	ITCACST A course of action to achieve short-term gains
TRANSFIXED	= 13.	XAIENTSFDR Made motionless
UNCOMPROMISINGLY	= 14.	MPUOLRCNONIIGMYS Unwilling to back down
BAFFLEMENT	= 15.	FTBALNEMEF Bewilderment

www.ingramcontent.com/pod-product-compliance
Lightning Source LLC
Chambersburg PA
CBHW051406070526
44584CB00023B/3320